CODEPENDENCY

How to Learn to Say No! The Complete Survival Guide for Overcoming Fear of Rejection & Abandonment and Increasing Self-Esteem in a Codependent Relationship

By
Melanie White

TABLE OF CONTENTS

INTRODUCTION 6
CHAPTER 1 WHAT IS CODEPENDENCY? 7
   How To Overcome Codependency? 8
CHAPTER 2 DO YOU KNOW WHAT CHARACTERIZES EMOTIONAL CODEPENDENCY? 11
   Codependency or altruism? 12
   Symptoms and characteristics of emotional codependency 13
   Self-esteem shines for its absence 14
   They seek to control the other person................14
CHAPTER 3 WHEN YOU LOVE TOO MUCH, MAYBE YOU DON'T LOVE 19
   Loving too much destroys us...............................22
   The masks in the couple 23
   When is it too much? 25
CHAPTER 4 ROPES THAT HURT 29
   Take the helm of your life 32
   Why we don't have the partner we want 33
CHAPTER 5 TOXIC LOVE IN THE RELATIONSHIP 37
   Differences Between Healthy And Toxic Love..42
   How to know if we are living in a "toxic relationship" as a couple? 46
   Clues of a toxic relationship 47

Get out of a toxic relationship 50
CHAPTER 6 DESTRUCTIVE BEHAVIORS IN A
RELATIONSHIP 52
　Destructive behaviors in the relationship........... 53
　The excuses that prolong emotional
　dependence 57
　What Are The Excuses That Prolong
　Emotional Dependence?....................................... 58
CHAPTER 7 SELF-CONTROL STRATEGIES IN
EMOTIONAL DEPENDENCE 63
　How far can emotional dependence go?............ 64
　Self-esteem and emotional dependence:
　communicating vessels 68
CHAPTER 8 HOW TO RECOGNIZE ABSORBING
RELATIONSHIPS... 73
　Types Of Couples 77
　7 Types of couples according to the
　triangular theory 79
CHAPTER 9 EMOTIONAL DEPENDENCE IN
ADOLESCENCE 82
　Emotional gaps... 86
CHAPTER 10 THE MEANING OF LIFE
ACCORDING TO VIKTOR FRANKL 91
　Existential vacuum: the feeling that life is
　meaningless 96
CHAPTER 11 PARTNER ABUSE 105
　Boiled Frog Syndrome... 109

Open your eyes and know yourself 112
CHAPTER 12 EXERCISES THAT WILL IMPROVE
YOUR RELATIONSHIP 114
  Habits That Help You Improve Your Sex Life 117
CHAPTER 13 LOVE, A CONSCIOUS CHOICE 122
  The balm of emotional dependence 125
  Five masked control mechanisms 129
CHAPTER 14 THE RELIEF OF LETTING GO OF
CONTROL 135
  Useless perfectionism 139
CHAPTER 15 HOW TO WORK ASSERTIVE
COMMUNICATION IN THE COUPLE? 143
  Intolerance to frustration in relationships 147
CHAPTER 16 THE CONSEQUENCES OF
ALCOHOLISM IN THE RELATIONSHIP 152
CHAPTER 17 THE PLASTICINE SYNDROME 157
CONCLUSION 161
TO LOOK FOR LOVE IS TO FIND YOURSELF 161

INTRODUCTION

Codependency is a multidimensional condition that can be called the most common addiction that people develop. The codependent person is addicted to a destructive pattern of relating with others. It is mainly characterized as a pattern of behaviors for maintaining an affective dependency relationship with a person, which in turn is controlled for an object of dependency and may or may not be of the emotional type. (Pérez and Delgado, 2003). Hence the importance of addressing Codependency in dating relationships.

From the theoretical perspective, this phenomenon has been studied through the psychosocial model whose primary representative is Erickson (1992), who mentions that in adolescence, there is a normative crisis, that is, a normal phase of conflict increase, where the more important task is to build a coherent identity and avoid confusion of roles.

According to the study by Gayol and Ramos (2002), a significantly higher percentage of codependency was found in women whose partners abused alcohol and mistreated them compared to those women who did not have these problems.

CHAPTER 1
WHAT IS CODEPENDENCY?

«Freedom means responsibility; that is why most men are so afraid of him.

(George Bernard Shaw)

Codependency is a psychological condition in which a person becomes emotionally attached to another. This is not, in any way, positive.

Why can't you make a decision yourself? Why do you need to have everything under control, and when something escapes you, the world comes upon you? If that person is missing, what do you do? A codependent person has every one of these fears.

A codependent person is...

- **Insecure**

The codependent person lives for others and abandons himself. He relies on the decisions of others, feeds on the opinions of the rest of the people, and is undervalued.

For the codependent person, the others are more important. He will always ask questions such as,

"What would they do in my place?" "How would they act?" He is not able to think for himself.

- **Controller**

As we have seen, the codependent person always needs someone to help hi make decisions, live, and even be happy. Since he cannot live without this, he will become controlling and manipulative to keep everything and everyone under his control. He doesn't want anyone to leave his side; he can't do without them!

- **Doubt yourself**

The codependent person cannot face the world, life, and even himself. He even doubts knowing how to live without having to depend on someone emotionally. How to do it? It is impossible for him.

His insecurity and fears make him unable to decide. Coping with life without a shoulder to lean on will cause terror and anxiety such that he will look for someone who meets this need.

How To Overcome Codependency?

If we feel attached to someone who is the center of our world, the reason for our existence and without which we cannot develop in life, is it possible to change this? Can we overcome being codependents? The answer is yes.

-Why do you feel that your life is not worth it? What makes you feel that it is impossible not to depend on anyone? Look inside you for what makes you feel inferior, reflect, and think about whether this is the case or not. You are not worth less than anyone. Why not start over?

-As a codependent person, your thoughts will be plagued by phrases such as "I don't know," "I can't do it," "He'll know how to do it. " Eliminate these thoughts, and if they surface, counteract them.

Nobody knows everything; nobody knows how to do everything. But there is something we can all do: learn. There is something I do not know? Well, I learn how. What can you not do? Are you sure about it? Have you tried it? Do not seek help; do not rely on another person. Try to be independent.

-Many circumstances surpass us, but it happens to all of us! The good thing is to know how to solve them, and overcome them ourselves. We cannot think of relying on another person, because that support may become unstable. Are we looking for another stronger support? No. Nothing will be better than being assured of our help.

-You know what you stand out in, your strengths! Well, what are you waiting for to exploit them? Work on them to learn to value yourself and not need to depend on anyone.

-Look for a reason for joy every day. You shouldn't care what others do, what matters is what you do. Stop looking at others as a model. Each one is unique. Make your life unique. Don't be codependent!

-Persevere. It is difficult, yes, but not impossible. Continue forward. You will not always have someone to lean on and when that happens, will the world come to you? You are reliable, intelligent, responsible...

You don't need to notify anyone; you don't need someone to live. Live your life, value yourself, be unique. Your life does not need to depend on anyone other than yourself.

Are you codependent? If so, I hope these and other tips can be of help. Although the best advice is your willpower, don't let yourself depend on someone! Experience the freedom of not being codependent.

CHAPTER 2
DO YOU KNOW WHAT CHARACTERIZES EMOTIONAL CODEPENDENCY?

Codependency involves an addiction to the dependence of another person, which can occur both in relationships, as well as within the family: for example, between a mother and a daughter. Thus, regardless of context, in very marked codependency relationships, the dependent person feels that he needs the other, just as he needs his heart to continue living. We will talk about a psychological dependence in which the emotional part is very involved.

In this sense, dependence goes beyond the mere desire to be next to someone. It has to do with thinking that the other is essential or irreplaceable to feel good—his presence is a necessary condition for this to happen. It is a need that must be met in any way, however particular and specific, that leads to happiness.

Emotional dependence is often coupled with jealous behaviors, manipulation, or possession of the loved one. This leads to the wearing out of the latter, who ends up leaving the relationship and realizing the irrational belief of the dependent; namely: without you, I am nothing.

In other situations, it is not only one member of the couple who is attached to the other, but it is both that depend, only in a different way. We enter, in this sense, what comes to be called emotional codependency.

What happens in a codependent relationship is that there is a dependent member whose happiness depends, ultimately, on their partner being by their side and not abandoning them. On the other hand, the other member of the couple is also dependent, but on the dependence of their partner.

Codependency or altruism?

To understand better, the dependent person needs their partner, and the codependent needs to protect, care, help, and care for the well-being of their partner. Taking actions in the relationship is indeed extremely necessary to keep it afloat, as long as they are done humanely, for love towards that person and not to feed an underlying dependency.

The only thing that the behaviors derived from codependency generate is the strengthening of the dependence between the two and filling internal gaps that have not been duly satisfied in childhood.

It is as if ensuring the safety of the other, protecting him excessively, or taking care of him as if he did not have the resources to do so in some way empowered the codependent couple and strengthened their self-esteem. Also, this way of acting is the water that quenches the thirst of the dependent, so the pieces of the puzzle end up fitting perfectly and causing the dependence to be reinforced frequently.

A toxic vicious circle is then created within the relationship: the happiness of one depends on the other person, and in turn, the joy of the latter depends on the need for attachment of the first. It may seem strange, but studies tell us that this is how some couples form or survive.

What is the ultimate result of this dynamic? The codependent couple never experiences a healthy and satisfying relationship, but suffering and the feeling of emptiness within the relationship become protagonists. In the rare case that the relationship is maintained over time, both have to endure a tremendously intense discomfort, since they end up losing even their own identity.

Symptoms and characteristics of emotional codependency

Although the protective person may seem healthy, the truth is that he is not. Actually, in the couple's care behaviors, he finds the only way to take care of his self-esteem. So, if you want to learn more about the symptoms of emotional codependency, read on.

Self-esteem shines for its absence

As we said before, codependent people tend to have low self-esteem that they try to replace with the sense of utility which can have real knowledge for others, in this case, for their partner.

In many cases, this lack originates from an anxious attachment pattern that began to form in childhood, in the relationship he established with his central reference figures. In this sense, it was easy for them only to reward him when he did something for them. From there, he learned that his value solely depended on what he was able to contribute to others.

They seek to control the other person

Since their self-esteem depends on the need for the other, they tend to use manipulation and control as a way to ensure that "their victim" does not escape. That is, to feel valuable and useful, they need the other person to continue to maintain their dependent behaviors, and this can only be assured by controlling the other.

Another common strategy to maintain dependence on the other is to undermine their self-esteem. Yes, make the other person feel invalid or useless so that he needs someone to come to the rescue. It is then that she appears, apparently selflessly and sacrificing herself.

They fear each other's independence

When they realize that the other person has taken a more independent action, such as making a decision alone; they panic and try to restore the situation. Therefore, it is not uncommon for them to abandon what they are doing to help the other person and continue to maintain their superior position as protector of the other.

They fear that the other will get it on their own and realize that they don't need anyone's help or that there are other people, apart from the codependent person, who can help them.

They become obsessed with the ir partner

In their heads, their partner is a focus of constant supervision. In this way, they become obsessive, end up losing themselves, and believe that facilitating the life of their partner is the only mission from which they can obtain well-being. Also, if they make a mistake in this regard, they are hardly forgiven, and frustration floods them.

They need too much approval

The approval of others is a universal reinforcement and in many cases, a sound source of information to evaluate our performance, but when we place all our self-esteem in the judgment that others can issue, we have a problem. In this sense, codependent people have a great need for approval that they try to cover. And who better to give immediate approval than the dependent person?

They feel responsible for each other's emotions

Although we know that the emotions of others do not belong to us, many times, we can feel guilty for how others think. It is not uncommon; we have been educated in this regard. "Don't make dad mad," "If you do, mom will be sad."

However, this thought is much more marked in codependent people: they believe that the other is right or wrong, depending on how they have acted. Thus, on many occasions, they end up carrying responsibilities that do not belong to them or guilt for something that was never in their hands.

They usually reproach their partner

On the one hand, they need to feel useful in helping their partner or another person in their environment who is dependent on them. On the other hand, when their partner does something that contradicts this pattern, they tend to reproach them as a strategy to make the other feel bad and change their behavior. They usually say expressions of this type: "With everything I do for you, this is how you pay me," "You do not know what I sacrifice for you," "I have left everything to make you happy," etc.

The concept of emotional codependency was expressly created to classify all those who showed emotional disturbances as a result of their partners as suffering a disorder related to substance. For example, drug addiction or alcoholism. Given this variability, currently, the personality pattern of this type of person cannot be clearly defined.

However, the characteristics that have been described in this chapter do allow us to identify some salient features of this emotional codependency. In addition to all of them, other less striking, but particular to this poor adaptation are personal neglect and self-annulment, together with shallow confidence and self-esteem. And these people usually have a history of romantic, individual, and emotional relationships characterized by their toxicity.

Identified with any of the parties? Although this way of acting in the relationship may surprise us, it is more common than we can imagine. Therefore, if you could identify with any of these traits, analyze what is failing, give your self-esteem a chance, and dare to experience a healthy relationship.

CHAPTER 3
WHEN YOU LOVE TOO MUCH, MAYBE YOU DON'T LOVE

Some tolerate and justify the abusive or toxic behavior of another, saying that they do it because they love them too much. What lies deep down is a codependent stance, born of deep insecurity and fear of abandonment.

Some people are willing to do anything or endure any humiliation in the name of love. They start from the premise that when one loves too much, there must be, above all, self-denial. That is, provide affection without conditions and forgive a thousand and one times if necessary. All in order not to lose or dislike the loved one.

Within that group of people are, for example, mothers who pay again and again the debts that their children contract. They know that this is not correct, but they end up justifying it in the name of love. There are also those people who embrace the same partner who mistreats them. They never leave them or leave them alone to return a short time later. They argue that when you love too much, no offense can break that bond.

The truth is that in cases like this, we are not facing a great love, but rather a dependency. This leads a person to experience a kind of affection that is overflowing and unmanageable. They feel they cannot live without the other. That is why they are willing to do anything except break that link. In these cases, you don't love yourself too much, but you lack love for yourself.

"The victim depends on the aggressor; there is emotional dependence. But it is that the aggressor also depends on the victim because he bases his self-esteem on domination."

-Ana Isabel Gutiérrez Saralegui-

Do you love too much, or do you need too much?

A codependent person, without realizing it, acts on a principle: I need you to need me. That is his way of building meaningful bonds in life. His essential attitude is to "rescue" the other, to serve as a buffer for any adverse consequences arising from the acts of that other.

This is accompanied by a perspective in which the other person does not matter. Their needs and desires should always be in the background. The only thing that matters is the needs and desires of the codependent. They are willing to sacrifice for them. They explain this unfair situation by merely saying that when you love too much, the limits on delivery disappear.

However, this situation causes them suffering and anxiety, mainly. When you love too much, likely, you will also have difficulty sleeping or experience a state of constant restlessness, eating disorders, or problems in other areas. They say that they love the other, but sooner rather than later, they turn their care and dedication into control behaviors, oriented in the background to keep that person tied.

I need you to need me

The distinctive feature of codependency is that on the one hand, there is someone who wishes to feel intensely useful or, rather, needed. This cannot be achieved with someone autonomous and mature. It requires a fragile person with many problems. Then a bond is formed when, on one end, there is someone with deficiencies and difficulties who does not want to take responsibility for himself. And on the other end, there is a codependent, who, in one way or another, assumes that responsibility belongs to him.

What emerges from this is an insane symbiosis—a type of relationship in which there is an abuse of side and side. In the end, there is a tacit agreement: the one "commits" not to solve his problems and the other to prevent him from doing so, in exchange for an unconditional "love." It is a neurotic entanglement that is challenging to recognize and analyze for those involved.

Therefore, the codependent feeds the abusive behaviors of the dependent—their excesses of consumption, anger, passivity, or whatever. Also, their excessive demands. What terrifies the codependent most is if the other stops needing him. In his imagination, if this were to happen, that person would probably depart from his side, for they would no longer need his protective mantle.

When you love yourself too much, perhaps what is in the background is a deep fear of abandonment. In this type of "love," suffering prevails, not happiness. They are common in people who have unprocessed childhood abuses. It results in such a situation when it is recognized that much of what is felt and done is not the fruit of love, but fear. Also, when those involved decide to cultivate self-esteem instead of projecting the lack in another.

Loving too much destroys us
When we talk about love, it seems that "more" is always synonymous with "better," and to believe this

lie is to take a poisonous pill disguised as caramel. If we analyze the moments lived with the person we want and the moments of suffering abound, we have become victims of what they call "love. "

To love is not to suffer; it is not to continually sacrifice and always bet on black. To love is not to be blind, it is not to justify the unmentionable or forgive any act for mercy. To love is not to depend; it is not to develop an umbilical cord that chains you to your partner.

Loving is not just a matter of quantity but quality. To love is not to overprotect, it is not to go back solving all the problems that the other sows nor to protect among children a child trapped in an adult body. And, of course, to love is not to end up physically or mentally torn; if our relationship impairs our emotional balance and even, perhaps, our health and physical integrity, we undoubtedly love excessively.

"That the love of a couple expects nothing in return is an invention of the submissive: if you give, you want to receive. It's healthy, reciprocal.

-Walter Riso-

The masks in the couple

It seems that a vast chasm between men and women separates the way of understanding and facing relationships. Cultural ideals, the education received, the family environment in which you grew up, and even the biology itself are actively involved.

Children's experiences with their reference figures and especially with their parents, play a fundamental role in how they interact with others throughout their lives. Painful and challenging situations, emotional deficiencies, absence of essential figures, or lack of limits are just some of the factors that mark the way we seek and care.

On the one hand, some women tend to handle love by developing a strong dependence or obsession for the other person. The torrent of emotions is lived very intensely, expressed through the need for care and understanding towards the other, and adopting the role of "savior" on many occasions. Thus, it is quite ironic that women can respond with such compassion to others and remain with a blindfold in the face of the pain of their own lives.

«If an individual is capable of loving productively, he also loves himself; if he only knows how to love others, he doesn't know how to love at all.»

-Erick Fromm-

On the other hand, many men escape their emotions through externalizing forms, that is, obsessing with their work, using drugs, or turning their free time into hobbies that leave little time to think. They are usually emotional blocking strategies due to their inability to manage and understand them. They do not cope with discomfort or problems because they pose an unmanageable, overwhelming, shameful, or blaming burden, which is best avoided.

This type of behavior can occur in both men and women, but it is generally women who develop patterns of care and sacrifice as a way of seeking and offering affection, while men try to protect themselves and avoid pain through more external than internal objectives, more impersonal than personal.

When is it too much?
Many times we are not satisfied with a partner, but we deny reality by saying that it is only a bad time. We justify the experience thinking that this is how relationships are, passionate in the beginning, and tortuous to the end.

We forgive each other's actions by convincing ourselves that it will change. Or maybe we don't dare to break the relationship "for fear of hurting." Actually, behind all this is our fear of suffering, we are afraid of being alone or of not finding another person who can stand us.

Have you ever fallen in love, and the feeling was not reciprocal? Or maybe you had excellent, heady sex that made no sense, but the rest of the relationship was an ordeal. Perhaps you have discovered yourself acting like a mother with your partner, or you think that without a person by your side, nothing makes sense.

The situations that we have been able to live with when we interact with other people are very diverse, and therefore there are also many mistakes we make and forms of self-deception that we invent to soften the pain.

"Guilt, shame, and fear are the immediate motives of deception."

-Daniel Goleman-

Maybe if we stop to analyze how we act with someone and how our partners usually act with us, we can find pieces that resemble each other, chapters that are repeated over and over again, even if it is a different person. Partners come and go in our lives, but we stumble upon the same stones.

There comes the point where we are immersed in a vicious circle, which only repeats itself. We are unable to leave and do not even know how we got there. Again the same dramatic melody, the same bitter chords, and although the orchestra is different, the conductor is still you. Although the person is different, although the vital moment you are in is different, although you promised not to go through the same thing again, there you are again, loving too much, and also severely.

The traces of the past

Why does this happen to us? The patterns we learn at an early age to relate to others are very fixed. We have been practicing them for a lifetime, and trying to abandon or change them is threatening and a terrible challenge. But it is more challenging to realize and be aware of the reality of the situation, to be able to see from within everything that is happening.

The key is to begin to understand each other, to ask ourselves why we continuously look for someone to care for or protect, why our voice is cut off when we try to explain what we feel, and end up abandoning the task. Why do I need to know what the other person is doing and control them when they are not next to me or why, despite the suffering, do we continue to maintain a relationship that is dead?

If our way of relating hurts us and hurts the person next to us, but we do nothing to understand and change it, life will not be a way to grow but a struggle to survive. If loving is painful, it is time to love yourself to stop the pain.

"Loving oneself is the beginning of a story of eternal love."

-Oscar Wilde-

CHAPTER 4
ROPES THAT HURT

Emotional dependence can become a real problem. When life revolves exclusively around another person, when there is no longer a space of its own, it is time to consider breaking the chains.

We understand codependency as a love that hurts. What irony, right? Something as beautiful as loving someone can suddenly become an ordeal.

This happens when we tie a person in a way we shouldn't. When we have not yet become aware that nobody belongs to us, but since childhood, we are taught that there is a kind of "property." Now I am yours, and you are mine, and vice versa. This is something we must start to change.

When love hurts

In all relationships between two people, conflicts will always arise. This is something natural, until it goes too far. When our partner begins to be the center of our all, when we develop codependency, since without it, we cannot manage to live our lives healthily, then we face a real problem.

That two people decide to share their life, love, respect, and live together, does not imply that they should depend on each other. Of course, they must continue respecting their spaces, and if the relationship does not work at any given time, nothing happens!

Our life cannot depend on anyone, it is only ours, and putting it in the hands of another person is almost like suicide. Therefore, you must consider what characterizes codependent people:

- Your self-esteem always depends on what your partner can or cannot tell you.
- You assume responsibilities that go far beyond your own, to try to meet the needs of your partner.
- There is an absence of boundaries between the self and the other in the relationship.
- You do not oppose your partner for fear of rejection.
- When a relationship ends, it is immediately immersed in another.

If you have identified with some of these characteristics, you have probably suffered or been close to suffering from emotional dependence.

Release the ropes that imprison you

Do you know what it's like when you are grabbing a rope so that it does not slip from your hands? If, as soon as you release it, the rope escapes from your hands, the effort you are making right now will probably damage your hands!

The same is happening in your head in a situation of codependency. You are tying someone to a relationship that is not doing you any good. We are not going to say that it does not cost to release the rope, but sometimes we are somewhat masochistic, and we prefer to endure the atrocious pain that we are going through.

If you hesitate to release the rope, or if you are clear that it would be best to release it, but you do not see yourself capable or find it complicated, it is a good time to do it once and for all.

But ... does this make you happy? It should be an unusual situation, but you're not satisfied—it hurts. You cannot continue to let this wilt you; you must free yourself from those ropes. Only you are holding that suffering; nobody is forcing you except yourself.

Take the helm of your life

Once you make the decision, the liberation you will feel cannot even describe it. You will be filled with inner peace. It is clear that right now, you are afraid, insecure, your self-esteem shines because of your absence, and your confidence lies in that person who has the highest respect.

Of course, it is difficult to take the step, so if you do not see yourself trained for it, seek help. Without it, you may not have the courage to face all this alone.

At this point, it is convenient to review and ask yourself what has led you to this. Is there a problem in my past that could have caused this fear of losing someone? Does love surpass me?

Sometimes love is like a drug. It is reasonable to think of that person, to feel desires to be with her at all times... Emotional dependence causes you to get down, to humble yourself if necessary, to get him to continue with you.

And if he leaves you? You immediately look for a substitute or replacement. This is a severe problem; you don't know how to be alone! You need that drug that makes you feel good, even if you have to crawl if necessary.

Seek help, speak it, open your eyes to reality. It will cost, you will get it, you will suffer (but were you not already suffering?). You will pass the withdrawal syndrome, and it will be just you again.

Learn to be alone, reconcile yourself with loneliness. He doesn't have to make you feel insecure and lonely in this world. You are your best company.

Why we don't have the partner we want

Many times, the partner we want does not resemble anything we have. Is it because of nonconformity, not knowing how to choose or looking for the negative things?

We cannot always have the partner we want, and that is due to many reasons. However, we have the possibility of being happy with the other person and especially with ourselves. Keep reading this chapter to learn more.

How is the partner we want?

First of all it is very important to take the time to think a little and reflect on what we like and what we don't, about a partner. Surely you have the ability to realize what makes you feel good and what bothers you or hurts you.

In this way, it will be easier, if you look for a relationship, to find someone who meets or even exceeds expectations. But be careful, because many times we believe that to fall in love we must meet the ideal person, the prince of the stories or the heroines of the comics and we end up alone for a long time.

Knowing what we want is perfect, but being realistic will help us find love without much pretense. That does not mean that we do not value ourselves or anything like that, but that the man or woman without defects does not exist, or only appear in novels and movies.

We cannot give you a recipe or a magic solution; you and no one but you have the ability to determine what you want in this life. It is essential to set aside myths; the 'half orange' is not realistic, because nobody arrives to fill in what we need (or at least it shouldn't be like that).

Why don't we have the partner we want?

Believe it or not, we all have the person we want next to us. Or that at least we wanted at some point and it seemed to us that nobody could match him or beat him. But, with the passage of time we realized how things really are and that what seemed to be beautiful and eternal is not so much anymore.

And that's when the problems begin, the fights, the recriminations and the separations. Maybe we don't have the partner we want because we fear asking him to change what makes us suffer. Or because we don't dare to follow our path alone.

Worst of all, we endure and let time pass, until one day we realize that we have spent our lives with someone who really did not make us happy.

On the other hand, it is very important to keep in mind that if we are not satisfied with our relationship, it may not be due to the relationship itself, but to how we are.

This means that if we have placed all our expectations on the other person, if we have believed the fairy tale and think that only that person is able to make us feel good, then we are likely to get frustrated, angry and distressed.

Also, if you are not satisfied with yourself, it is almost impossible for you to be satisfied with those around you; and that includes a partner but also friends, family, work colleagues, etc.

And of course, we cannot ignore the constant pressure that the family or society puts on us. It is mandatory to be happy, to have the perfect partner and to comply with all cultural commandments.

Why do we want something different in a partner?

People are dissatisfied by nature and that has something good if we know how to handle it. Otherwise, we suffer too much ... and it's not worth it.

When we are alone we want to find someone to do certain activities with, but when we have a partner the most we do is go to the movies, dinner or the beach on a weekend. We loved that this person we met was so independent , but then it bothers us that he goes out with his friends so much.

We were happy to share our love of series and movies. But now, we get bored that this is the only plan of the weekend ... We could give thousands of other examples.

It is said that people want what they do not have instead of enjoying what they do have. It may seem difficult to understand, but it is simpler than you think.

We miss what we don't have for a dose of anxiety and 'futurism' that we don't know how to control. And instead, we should take a break, look around and be thankful for everything we have, including someone to love.

CHAPTER 5
TOXIC LOVE IN THE RELATIONSHIP

We often think that the worst thing that can happen to a relationship is that it doesn't work, despite having love. This is not true, the most harmful thing that can happen to a couple, as in any relationship, is that what no longer works takes one more step towards the negative pole and becomes toxic.

By toxic, we mean harmful. It is no longer about the relationship providing well-being to each of its members, but it begins to subtract it. It functions as a kind of acid that damages each one individually, turning the two into a sort of brake for growth.

Toxic love in the relationship

Poisonous love is an emotional pain that is born from the heart of the union itself, from the committee that becomes poisonous. A toxic relationship is like a weakened spirit that needs another person to be able to nourish and survive because, on its own, it does not believe it is capable of doing so. This type of "love" is an emotional pain that can destroy all the right parts of a person until there is nothing left but a void.

Toxic love hides behind a smokescreen where people deceive themselves, thinking that their partner »is not wrong» and try to see only the positive parts, such as "he is a protective person," "I love him above all things," and that takes care of him. However, the reality is that the relationship is only based on uncertainty, anger, need, insecurity, and even suspicion.

A person who is too long in a toxic love relationship will lose sight of what is a healthy relationship... he will forget it and think that what happens to him is normal, but nothing is further from reality. A love relationship is based on respect and building a path together, full of good times that will make both parties feel happy.

«Disturbing emotions and toxic relationships have been identified as risk factors that favor the appearance of some diseases.»

-Daniel Goleman-

Any relationship can become a toxic relationship if couples do not take care of their emotional health. Being with a toxic person can lead to a serious love relationship. That is why you must keep in mind that there are things that you can never tolerate, under any circumstances in your relation. Because love is not always unconditional, and if your partner does not behave well, you should seek help immediately.

You despise or disrespect yourself

John Gottman, one of the most recognized experts in the field of couple psychology, states that when he observes couples, the first thing he looks at is contempt or disrespect in communication. Gottman says that contempt or disrespect are definite signs that continuity in the pair is at a critical point.

John Gottman often comments that contempt or disrespect includes sarcasm, cynicism, insults, voluntary attentional ignorance, mockery, or hostile humor. This usually occurs when there is a lack of respect from your partner and the problems are not resolved. The relationship is destroyed as well as your self-esteem, if you have a person next to you who despises you.

Puts you last

Health, children, and work are priorities in everyday life, but the relationship should not be in the last position. If your partner ignores you, then there is a problem which will not let you move forward. This is known as partner negligence and is something real; this lack of interest is a murderer that is slowly killing your relationship. Two people who love each other should ensure that they meet their own emotional needs, but also that of their partner.

"In any relationship, if one person feels that the other is not putting anything on the table, he or she will begin to disrespect the other person."

- Sherry Argov-

You have been unfaithful

Infidelity is not something that should be tolerated especially when you take care of your relationship to the fullest every day. A healthy couple requires complete fidelity and does not seek emotions and experiences (not consented) in the arms of other people.

Cheating or infidelity can also occur when you talk badly about the relationship, or when you spend time alone with others of the opposite sex to flirt. Sometimes being unfaithful is not necessarily having sex with another person; being unfaithful is disrespecting your partner and the relationship you are building with them.

If you are physically or verbally abused

Words can cause an emotional wound just as a

beating would leave a bruise. Physical, verbal, and emotional abuse is not acceptable in any relationship and even less from a romantic partner. If your partner hits you, humiliates you, forces you to have sex against your will, or mistreats you, you should seek help as soon as possible.

Because before the abuse, of any kind... you should not hide or shut up, you deserve to find happiness inside and break the chains of a cage that hurts you.

It is time for a change

When a relationship has become toxic, it is time for a change. If despite the attempts to improve the relationship, nothing has changed, it is time to consider putting an end to this stage of our life. As painful as it may seem to us, sometimes we strive to follow relationships that sink us.

Learning to accept change is essential. Our partner is not an obligation but a choice in our life. As a general rule, the only thing that binds us to our commitment is our mind and our way of dealing with the situation. In the same way that we don't belong to our partner, they doesn't belong to us either. A relationship is formed by two free beings who have decided to share their path.

Continuing in a toxic relationship can only bring psychological problems and emotions to both members. Thus, carrying out an act of sincerity and recognizing that it is best to put an end to the relationship, will be the best decision. Our life does not revolve around a relationship, do not make the mistake of falling into it.

Differences Between Healthy And Toxic Love

There are healthy relationships where differences are tolerated and even celebrated. But, there are also toxic ones, where those differences are a threat to the relationship. In this chapter, we give you some keys to identifying the different links.

Love is one of the most intense feelings we can experience. If we have enough emotional maturity, this exaltation allows us to enjoy an incredible experience with our partner and enjoy healthy love.

If, on the contrary, our emotional maturity is not sufficiently formed, we can surrender to a toxic relationship believing that we must make a lot of sacrifices in the name of love.

We cannot deny that sharing our life with another person implies essential changes. However, we must know how to differentiate healthy behaviors from destructive ones.

And, although it is easy to overlook, there is a thin line between feeling love and having an emotional dependence or obsession for the other person. How can I differentiate it? Although it is difficult for many to accept, specific characteristics allow us to confirm what kind of love it is.

Healthy or toxic love?

Let's discover together the characteristics of both relationships so that you can determine if you are living one or the other.

1. Support

When love is healthy, there is much importance in the individual development of each party. Therefore, both seek to support and encourage when they want to reach a goal or go through a critical moment.

If the relationship is toxic, the couple acquires obsessive behavior and fears that the other person will fulfill a dream or be "superior" in certain aspects. This type of person will always seek to manipulate you to feel that he is in charge.

2. Acceptance

Accepting the defects of the other person is essential for every healthy relationship. It is necessary to take enough time to know them since love implies tolerating and respecting the other as they are.

If love is toxic, there will always be objections towards the other. In one way or another, the way to change their personality will be sought to fulfill their interests.

3. Freedom

For love to last, it is essential to respect each other's freedom. All people have separate interests that they do not always want to share with their partner.

An outing with friends, hobbies, or a work project are not reasons to generate a conflict. On the contrary, both accept that they are vital elements to nurture the relationship.

If there is emotional codependency, there is not enough confidence to do activities in which they are not together. The idea of not seeing what the other person is doing is cause for jealousy and insecurity.

4. Communication

This aspect can be decisive to differentiate a healthy relationship from a destructive one. While in a healthy relationship, each conversation is constructive, in a toxic one, conflicts and culprits are always generated.

When the couple has enough confidence to talk and solve their problems without the need to attack or manipulate each other, the type of love is healthy.

If anyone tries to become the victim or always pretends to be right, we must assess whether it is a toxic relationship.

5. Intimacy

The sexual field is one of the most critical components of any relationship. However, it is not necessary to sacrifice one's interests to please the partner.

If love is healthy and pure, intimacy arises from desire. The bond they have is so strong that there are no fears when expressing desires, tastes, or those actions that are uncomfortable in sex.

On the contrary, if there is not enough trust or manipulation, feelings of insecurity may arise when having sex. Either one sacrifices what they feel to meet the needs of the other.

6. Privacy

The privacy of the couple is an essential component that requires a lot of respect. Due to the trust that is formed between the two, it is common to discuss sensitive issues that should not be disclosed for any reason.

If there is enough maturity to cope with it, none will share these aspects with other people. If the relationship is toxic, these details are grounds for mocking or manipulating the other.

7. Happiness

A healthy relationship is made up of happy moments. Continuously both seek to share new experiences and adventures.

Despite the difficulties, the two feel that they complement each other and that there is nothing better in the world. In toxic love, it is difficult to experience these feelings. Most of the time, one suffers or feels limited to leave the comfort zone.

What kind of love do you identify in your life? If you consider your relationship to be toxic, analyze how to solve it so that it doesn't cause you more suffering. We all deserve to have healthy love that makes us feel full.

How to know if we are living in a "toxic relationship" as a couple?

You may still love your partner; however, in toxic relationships, something curious happens: when he is not with you, you rest. You find "air" and relax.

Sometimes love is not enough. What is even more dangerous is one who loves you in the worst possible way, making you unhappy and offering only jealousy and distrust. Do you think you have a toxic relationship? Continue reading.

It may seem to the naked eye that it is easy to recognize if we are living in a toxic relationship. But it is not. Hence we fall into them on more than one occasion. When we love a person, we suffer cognitive and emotional distortion, which is very difficult to "wake up" from.

Today, in our space, we invite you to know the most obvious clues.

Clues of a toxic relationship
1. See walls where you used to have doors

It is possible that before having a partner, you were a relatively independent woman. You had your job and made your own decisions. You stayed with your friends, went out with your coworkers, and calmly planned your daily routines.

But now:

- You can no longer decide what you want to do,

since you always have to agree with your partner. When you tell him that you are going to do something specific like attending a company dinner, or go shopping with a family member, it is common to get bans.

- **Your life has been coerced overnight.** Living at the epicenter of a toxic relationship can make one have to take special care of, for example, the style of clothing, the use of makeup, or the privacy of the mobile phone.
- You begin to see an explicit limitation in your future perspectives. It is possible that your partner does not agree that you are better at work. From one day to the next, you begin to see walls in illusions that were previously your own.
- Day by day, you see how an invisible shell is surrounding you.

2. Your emotional balance is violated

Many women begin an emotional relationship with great enthusiasm. Love is very intense, an emotion so overflowing, sincere, and full, where it is reasonable to offer everything of ours to the person we love. But remember, it is necessary to love with balance, always taking care of our self-esteem:

- A toxic relationship still has the fundamental pillar of emotional manipulation. And this is exercised in the most subtle and destructive ways.
- Toxic people always seek their main benefit. Always remember that every manipulative person has an insecure personality and low self-esteem. Such insecurity creates distrust and desire for control over the coupling. He is afraid of being abandoned, of others taking away the person he wants. And this leads to continuous surveillance and excessive jealousy...
- The desire for control generates in them a position of absolute power where only one exercises the right to make decisions. If you do not do what your partner asks you, he will use clever tricks to make you feel guilty, playing the victim, and making you believe that you are the culprit. You must be careful.

3. Unhappiness that grows day after day

You see, even with some envy, living with more harmony, where both respect each other's personal spaces and personal growth, is possible.

You notice a pressure inside. You feel dissatisfied, and everything that used to identify you is getting lost, fraying... You are not the who you were before. And you notice, your self-esteem has plummeted, and you perceive yourself a little broken inside.

You must take into account all this data. Frequently, this emotional weakness in which we have fallen ends up somatizing us.

What does this mean? That anxiety, fear, worry, becomes, for example, headache or back pain, nausea, chronic pain... Many women go to the doctor and do not get a proper diagnosis.

They can tell you, for example, that you suffer from migraines, but in reality, what you experience is a depression generated by your unhappiness.

Get out of a toxic relationship
It is curious, but statistical data tell us that a toxic relationship can last many years. How can this be possible? Basically, for the following aspects:

1. Because many women are afraid of the potential consequences of leaving their partner. They fear for their children, or that their spouse may harm them.
2. We must also bear in mind that there are people who do not conceive of "being without a partner." So they get carried away, so to

speak, they get carried away by that unhappiness because it will always be better than living alone.
3. Sometimes, these relationships last very long because the couple continues to love each other. They love each other badly. They cause each other harm, but they do not conceive of another form of existence. It is surprising, but it is true.

To get out of a toxic relationship, it is first necessary for you to be aware of what is happening. Understand that this way, you will not be able to be happy. Maybe your friends and family have noticed the clues long before you. Pay attention to them, seek support if you need it.

The second step will be to talk to your partner. Tell him what you feel, tell him about your feelings, your frustration, and your unhappiness. If you see that he does not do his part to improve the situation, if you perceive that there is no will to change ... get away.

Your integrity, peace of mind, and physical and emotional health come first, never doubt it.

CHAPTER 6
DESTRUCTIVE BEHAVIORS IN A RELATIONSHIP

A relationship is a link between two people that is necessary to cultivate and work on every day. It implies a daily coexistence and, as such, is susceptible to being immersed in different conflicts and discrepancies. If the members of the relationship do not act from love and respect towards each other to resolve these conflicts, the relationship may end up wilting.

Dr. John Gottman is one of the pioneers in the study of romantic relationships. After studying many couples for years, today, you can say that some certain destructive behaviors or attitudes are good predictors of failure.

On the other hand, some couples work very well as such. This again has to do with a series of common ingredients that predict the continuity in the couple's time, as well as their well-being. In any case, the parts that should never be lacking in a relationship, whatever the type, are: respect, affection, trust, and communication.

If we are in a relationship in which these ingredients are present, we will likely enjoy the relationship, regardless of the discussions or conflicts that sometimes arise. If, on the contrary, we notice that there are some missing elements, it is necessary for the couple to try to work on those points.

«Love is an activity, not a passive effect; it is a continued being, not a sudden start»

-Erich Fromm-

Destructive behaviors in the relationship

As we have said, there are certain behaviors in relationships that predict failure. In this section, we are going to point out the ones that seem most relevant to us and that directly attack the fundamental pillars that sustain every healthy relationship: respect, affection, trust, and communication:

Contempt. To despise the other means to put him in a position lower than you. It may involve other behaviors, such as humiliating, making destructive criticisms, not contributing anything to the other person or directly insulting and disrespecting them. When someone despises you and is something that is done repeatedly in the relationship, he does not love you. In this case, you must rethink if it compensates to continue in that relationship.

Ignore. It is one of the most destructive behaviors that exist. To ignore the other person when there is a conflict or discussion is to forget that this person—who is our partner and is supposed to be loved—has communication, expression, support, and other such needs. The ignored person can feel tremendously humiliated, and what usually happens in the long term is that the person ends up with a low self-esteem, even believing that he does not deserve the attention of the other or has done something wrong.

Cancel the other. If we are in a relationship where the other person tells us how we should be, what we should be interested in, what friends we should have, etc., they are canceling us. When a person loves another, he accepts them as they are, unconditionally. He is supposed to have chosen them precisely because of how they are. When someone pretends that the other person changes, he does not want that person anymore.

Codependency. This behavior is important. Some people are not able to leave a relationship because they feel they need their partner. They prefer to endure criticism, annulment, indifference so as not to be alone. In the same way, the other member feels reinforced because their partner depends on them. We enter, therefore, in the field of emotional codependency, something tremendously destructive that can lead to very negative consequences for the couple.

Never strive. We indeed have to be honest with our partner and show ourselves as we are, but sometimes it is also necessary to give in. For example, if our partner is asking us to accompany him to an event, even if we don't feel like it too much, we can make an effort. In the same way, other times, it must be our partner that compromises for us. In this sense, we demonstrate with actions that we love the other person and that sometimes, we don't mind sacrificing ourselves.

Why do we endure for so long?

Sometimes couples endure this type of destructive behavior for too long. Logically, sometimes, we make mistakes in the relationship, and it is healthy to be flexible and tolerant with the other member. Understand that they were wrong. The problem arises when it is something recurring, which defines the relationship. Think about how you would draw you and your partner. Hand in hand? Kissing? Arguing? The way you portray your partner considerably projects what is present in your mind about him.

If we are aware, even minimally, that our partner has become toxic, it is necessary to shuffle the pros and cons and be willing to let go. Most of the time, it is so hard for us to end the relationship because there is a widespread fear of loneliness. We think about loneliness catastrophically and not objectively. We believe that we are going to be alone when in reality, we are surrounded by people.

"Why, in general, is loneliness avoided? Because there are very few who find a company with themselves ».

-Carlo Dossi-

On the other hand, specific thoughts try to deceive us so as not to leave the relationship. A prevalent belief is, "It will surely change." Another very typical idea is, "If I leave the relationship, I'm sure he will find another person with whom he will do better." Try to ignore these thoughts. In reality, they are the result of our deep-seated fear of abandonment or loneliness and try to "protect us," but they produce the opposite effect.

The most sensible thing is to stop deceiving ourselves, objectively observe all the facts, as if we were a spectator of our relationship, and make a firm decision. Once this point has been overcome—the most complicated—we will have to be willing to go through the duel tunnel and arrive renewed for acceptance.

The excuses that prolong emotional dependence

The reasons we give ourselves when we suffer psychological dependence help us to postpone an almost inevitable and necessary end: reconciling with loneliness.

Emotional dependence is spread by a very intense and poorly developed attachment to a specific person. It usually is about the partner who is generally praised and idealized, believing that, without their existence, happiness would be impossible. On the other hand, several excuses prolong emotional dependence, making the person feel unable to part with it.

The dependent person harbors in their guts a series of nuclear schemes or beliefs that bring with them the fear or refusal to be left alone or the idea that one must rely on others, that alone they can do nothing, that others must make decisions with and for them.

By having these beliefs, people with emotional dependence see themselves as rather weak beings.

They underestimate their abilities and need to rely on another. This need to be with another person or to have a partner leads them to look for someone to fill that emptiness from which fear of loneliness emanates.

Your partner may disrespect you, be unfaithful or mistreat you; however, even if you want to break the thread for a moment, you feel like you cannot "detach" yourself. You know that you are suffering, and you would like your life to flow in another current, but neither one can change his or her attitude to stop the damage and begin to heal the wound.

In this sense, cognitive dissonance is created between what you should do for your good and what you are actually doing.

You know you have to leave; however, you stay every day. This is where the excuses that prolong emotional dependence arise, such as self-verbalizations to deceive ourselves and thus continue to cling to the person who harms us or a toxic relationship.

What Are The Excuses That Prolong Emotional Dependence?

Regarding emotional dependence, the excuses for not breaking the situation can be as many as there are dependent people. In this sense, it has been seen that there are certain harmful verbalizations that they enter into their internal dialogue or even come to share with others. They would be the following and would serve as excuses that prolong emotional dependence:

He will change

This excuse is a classic. To reject the idea that the person we have at our side is not the right one, we tell ourselves that they will change. But why would that person have to change? How are you sure he really will? If he has not already done so, what will be the stimulus that will make him change?

Therefore, instead of turning our backs on reality, it is better to assume that this person probably will not change and that we have two options: accepting it as it is—which, if we are suffering is not a good option—or end the relationship that unites us to them, although this involves going through a grieving process. .

Keep in mind that people are as they are and unless they decide to change their behavior or shape their way of being, the change will not come by magic.

I love him too much

We often believe that love is a motive that legitimizes everything. We say " love can do everything," and according to that idea, the dependent person begins to fit the blows. It doesn't matter if someone manipulates them, or disrespects them, the person keeps holding on because he understands that this is precisely a demonstration of love.

When we are well, everything is great

All couples have their good and bad times. The idea is to consider to what extent the bad moments exceed in frequency and intensity those in which the relationship seems to work well. If you notice that your partner's contempt, arguments, and toxicity are imposed on the decisive moments, you need to raise your head towards the horizon and ask yourself what you want to draw from it.

What if I am wrong to leave the relationship?

This is the perfect excuse that anyone with emotional dependence would give not to take that step to end the relationship. It is very close to that of "insurance that changes." Our desire for things to go differently makes us anchor ourselves in the illusion that the future will come better. So, I can't leave because I will miss that future. If you look, it is nothing more than a fiction that our brain creates so as not to have to go through a grieving process.

If your partner has not already made changes, if everything is always the same, if you have even been like that for years, if you have tried everything... what are you going to be wrong about? Isn't it possible that, instead, you are making a mistake now?

Now is not the time to speak

The perfect moment does not exist, just as there is no ideal way to communicate with our partner. The key is that we do it as soon as possible: we have already verified that it is a problem that will not be solved alone.

The possible moments to take that step forward are many, the promising ones, being a conversation that we don't want to have, are any. It's going to be his birthday; His parents just got separated; Christmas is just around the corner; How can I tell him now that it's our anniversary?

Think about whether these excuses are real reasons to postpone your desire to communicate something, or it is the fear of his reaction that signs the postponement.

The key is self-esteem

Getting rid of excuses that prolong emotional dependence is not easy; in a way, that's why we talk about "dependence." On the other hand, some factors position us as good candidates to shape a relationship of this kind; one of the most important is self-esteem.

A person looks in the mirror and does not identify reasons for someone wanting to maintain a relationship with him. Hence, he sees the relationship as a fortune, a "kind of luck" that he can try to keep paying a high price.

On the other hand, he also has moments of clarity in which he is aware that the same relationship he clings to is the one that is hurting him. It is in these moments that the excuses that prolong the emotional dependence appear; that is why it is so necessary to eliminate them from the internal dialogue.

In emotional dependence, there is one that is on top of a pedestal, and the other pals him from below because they think he is inferior.

CHAPTER 7

SELF-CONTROL STRATEGIES IN EMOTIONAL DEPENDENCE

Emotional dependence has some costumes that make it attractive. Forms that make us fall into it, to experience its unpleasant consequences later. In this chapter, we will talk about some strategies to resist its "charm."

Emotional dependence is one of the most frequent reasons for consultation, although clients or patients do not think in principle that this may be the reason. The prevalence is higher in women, although we do not know if this prevalence is real since the data is based on the frequency with which they go to the clinic for this reason.

When a patient suffers from emotional dependence, the psychologist does not usually suspect him, since he can hear how the patient verbalizes that "he loves his partner too much, " or "he will change over time when he becomes aware."

Although the person's needs are relegated to a second, third, or fourth level, the primary objective is that your partner does not despise you or is not absent from your side.

In this sense, the emotional dependent is capable of abandoning projects that are important to him, neglecting other people, spending excessive amounts of money on gifts, or even not setting limits on disrespect or humiliation on the part of his partner.

Some people go so far with their emotional dependence that they throw away their whole lives, this problem becoming generalized to their work, their family, or their social environment.

We can imagine how the self-esteem of these people is when they put their partner far above themselves, even if it hurts them. What happens is that there is an unresolved emotional lack that they try to fill with the ephemeral affection of another person.

For this reason, abandonment is so essential, since it would mean becoming orphans of love or affection, something that they lack alone.

How far can emotional dependence go?
When I explain emotional dependence, I usually draw a " puppet " running behind a heart with a hole in the center of his body—as if they were missing a piece. The hole, which also has a heart shape, can only be filled with Self-esteem, that is, with the heart that the patient places himself.

The clerk does not know this and thinks that running after a heart that is outside is the solution to his problem. And run, run and don't stop running, for days, months, even decades. What is the result of this demanding career? The only consequence that our " puppet " obtains is precisely exhaustion.

The heart is not reached, and if it is reached and we place it in our hollow, it does not help us. It is as if it is not our size. And the question that is essential to understand is that no heart will fit.

The only heart that can serve us, as we have said, is the one we give ourselves. And in this sense, power is not outside but born from within.

But, if we don't know this, the result is that we can go very far on that expedition. We can lose our friends by leaving them to avoid rejection from our partner; we can sabotage our values, tastes, hobbies to satisfy the other person. We can abandon jobs, trips, exciting projects because we don't want leave our partner, and that means their loss. We can even become jealous and try to control everything the other does, with the suffering that entails an unfortunate result.

What can we start doing to avoid falling into this trap?

Self-control strategies in emotional dependence

The techniques from the psychological point of view that we can carry out to gain self-control in an emotional relationship have to be aimed at managing our most passionate and entrenched impulses.

Emotionally dependent people, as with other agencies, know that their way of acting hurts them, but they cannot stop doing so because their "emotional GPS" is firm in guiding their actions.

It is difficult to break the dependent habit, but after all, it is only about that: a habit or a pattern learned and can be unlearned with determination.

Some ways to do this unlearning are:

When you are going to type a text message to your partner or ex-partner as an attempt to control, either by jealousy or by knowing what he thinks or what he is doing, you should write that same message on a blank page. In this way, you gain time—the emotion lowers its intensity in a few minutes—and you also force yourself to get it out of your mind before retyping it on your mobile.

This simple exercise can create "reactivity," and this is an advantage as it can inhibit you from finally doing the action.

Try to practice zero contact. If the relationship is over and you're still hooked, try reducing the actual connection to zero. Remove them from all social networks, avoid meeting friends in common or frequent places where you can run into one another.

If you feel the urge to go to his house, get close to talk to him, etc., do a contrary behavior. If to go to his home, you have to take the car and drive on a specific road, deviate to another alternative way that forces you to make many turns to reach your primary destination. As in the rest of the strategies, this will allow you to save time and think more rationally.

Think about what you will get by following your impulses. Will he come back to you? Will you get him to explain to you, as you want, why he is no longer by your side? Will you get him back with you? Do you want to return with him? If, after all the questions, you conclude that you are not going to come to anything other than an argument, fatigue or irritation that you could have saved yourself, reconsider if you still want to follow your instincts.

Make a reminder card. When you are emotionally calm, write a reminder card that you always have to carry with you to access it. There you have to write sentences that help you not to take the step to the dark side when you are too emotional. They have to be phrases that come to you and serve you.

An example could be: «You already have experience and know that acting in this way only ends up hurting you. Isn't that a good reason to keep the effort to control your impulses? »

Self-control in emotional dependence is difficult to acquire. It requires constant work and, even so, nobody is immune. We have to know that falls or relapses are part of the process, and continue to persevere.

Little by little, with practice, we will gain in self-esteem and stop getting involved in relationships based on dependence, to generate and maintain healthy, smooth, and fluid relationships.

Self-esteem and emotional dependence: communicating vessels

We are social beings. We like to please and share things with others. But can this need for approval be harmful to us? Here is one of the keys to emotional dependence. Do you have to like everyone or just those important to you? Who are the relevant people in your life? Do they have to approve absolutely everything you do?

I invite you to ask yourself these questions and try to answer them. It is one thing to be clear about what you want to do and know that you would like your loved ones to approve it and another to feel that if everyone does not love you, things are not worth it ... The difference though subtle is still essential. Read on to learn how all this influences your well-being!

«If you are not good at loving yourself, you will have a hard time loving someone because you will resent the time and energy you give to another person that you do not even give yourself.»

-Barbara De Angelis-

What is emotional dependency?

People with emotional dependence excessively need the affection, attention and approval of others. They feel an irrational fear of loneliness and abandonment, which will make them more subordinate in their interpersonal relationships. Also, they have a strong desire for exclusivity and report that they could not imagine life without their partner.

They, therefore, present a persistent pattern of emotional needs that they are unable to satisfy themselves, so they intend to cover them by establishing inappropriate ties with other people. That is, they develop parasitic and asymmetric relationships, carrying out acts of all kinds and conditions and that justify with a single purpose: that the relationship does not end.

«The worst loneliness is not being comfortable with yourself.»

-Mark Twain-

And not only that. They crave feelings of protection and affection with such intensity that they look for it in the other person in such a way that they cancel themselves regardless of the quality of the relationship in order to maintain it. Thus, they establish links that are very intense and unstable rather than healthier ones. We all like to feel loved, but ... we are not willing to do just anything to get it.

How does emotional dependence influence psychological distress?

The problem of being emotionally dependent—in excess—on others is that, if they do not receive the attention or the excessive love we need, there are irrational doubts about our worth and the appreciation that others have for us, which will influence our self-esteem and the emotions we feel.

Thus appear feelings of rejection, denial, and abandonment. In this way, sadness is present too intensely, which can lead to us entering a vicious circle of emotional emptiness and chronic dissatisfaction from which it is tough to get out: depression.

But not only that, the fear of being alone that leads people to do anything to avoid loneliness, makes anxious symptoms increase. The person anticipates the possibility of this happening, which makes him very nervous and engages in toxic emotional relationships.

Against emotional dependence: self-esteem

As you can imagine, people with emotional dependence have low self-esteem and see themselves negatively. This leads, again, to a greater need to seek support and affection in others. In other words, to be well, they need others to be well with him or her.

The reality is that the only person we spend our entire lives with is ourselves. Therefore, it is essential to base our well-being on seeking our approval and not that of everyone else. What do I mean by this? That the first person we try to please with what we do must be ourselves.

«People who want more approval get less, and people who need less approval get more.»

-Wayne Dyer-

But what else can we do to like ourselves more? A straightforward exercise would be to look every day for something that has made us feel good, both physically and psychologically. In the beginning, it is a task that will cost us since we are not accustomed to flattering ourselves, but in the long run, we will foster positive affection with our person. In this way, we will reduce pathological emotional dependence. Love yourself!

CHAPTER 8
HOW TO RECOGNIZE ABSORBING RELATIONSHIPS

Absorbent relationships do not give us space to grow, be happy, or enjoy outside the other person's environment. They are so toxic that they lower us, depress us, and reduce our self-esteem.

Some believe that lack of self-esteem leads us to star in absorbing, toxic, and complicated relationships. That 'need' to spend all day with your partner can be synonymous with love, but also emotional dependence. Once we have passed the initial infatuation stage, in which everything revolves around that beautiful being beside, everyone should have their own activities and spaces.

Keys to recognize absorbing relationships

It is effortless to confuse love and passion with dependence. And with time, there are clear signs that the person with whom you have decided to share your days absorbs all your energies, free hours, and activities. Pay attention to these signs of absorbing relationships:

1. You stop having autonomy

As we said, it is normal that at first, you want to stay as long as possible with the other person. However, after the initial phase, the first signs of the absorbent relationship begin.

In this way, the loss of autonomy translates into not going to any event without 'company.' Or reducing contact with other people (friends or family) by spending time with the other person. Social life must be maintained, even if it is cut.

The lack of autonomy can also be experienced when all plans are intended for the couple, and there is no room for anything individual. Even when we don't like watching sports or a romantic movie, we do it to be together.

2. You receive messages and calls continuously

It is nice to hear a few romantic words in the morning or before bedtime, but when the messages or calls become 'bombing,' it is not pleasant, especially if they modify or create problems in other environments, such as work or study life.

Sweetness and passion become empalago and annoyance when they are excessive. If he calls you every five minutes 'because he wants to know how you are' or 'because he can't live without hearing your voice,' it can be a serious problem and, without a doubt, a typical sign in absorbing relationships.

3. You have no privacy

You have given your partner your social media, email, and mobile passwords... They read the messages that your friends leave you, and have to know who is calling you. Not having privacy is synonymous with being in a toxic and suffocating relationship.

Your partner does not have to go with you on every birthday party or event. Especially if the other boyfriends or girlfriends will not go. Nor do they have to accompany you if you want to buy clothes or have an appointment with the doctor.

It may seem nice that they want to spend most of their time with you, but everyone must have their own life. This does not mean that you do not want or love him less, but we all need a little air, freedom, and time to do what we like.

4. They organize the agenda

It is hazardous for your partner to tell you what to do and, above all, that for each activity he must accompany you. Each one has his tasks, his obligations, and his commitments and, although we can dedicate time to enjoy as a couple, only you can organize your agenda.

5. Be careful

It is said that jealousy is synonymous with love. However, in some cases, we must be cautious because they are typical signs of absorbing relationships.

A very jealous person is not sure of himself, believes that the other will deceive him at the first carelessness, stop loving him, or find someone better and abandon him forever.

The jealousy can occur anytime, anywhere: with your group of friends, your colleagues, your gym teacher, a neighbor, or even with your family. Do not accept this type of behavior, as it can get worse over time.

At first, you are likely to listen to him to please him, but then you will later regret having allowed those attributions. Nobody has no right to tell you how to dress, who to see, who to work with, or what to study. Much less make a jealous scene in front of others!

6. Conditions are always imposed

Finally, another of the signs in absorbing relationships is the pressure that a person exerts on his partner.

"Choose between your friends/colleagues/work/study / family or me" is a very typical expression.

Being in that situation is quite tricky because, on the one hand, we want to spend time with those we love the most, but on the other, we cannot neglect our goals, dreams, or desires.

What this 'absorbent' person does not understand is that by acting in this way, the only thing he achieves is to moving further away from your life, not the opposite. Just think about the type of relationship you have, you will not hesitate to leave him.

Types Of Couples

According to Sternberg's "theory of love," there are seven types of couples that are the result of combining the three essential elements: intimacy, passion, and commitment.

Love is possibly one of the most complex issues that brings us more headaches. Many human beings seek to mate and share their life with someone special, but achieving it in practice can be very difficult.

Therefore, psychology has been studying phenomena such as love, attraction, and relationships for decades. Although there have been many discoveries in this field, one of the models that best explain the seven types of couples is Sternberg's theory of love.

The triangular theory of love: what it is

After studying the behavior of a good number of couples, Sternberg created a model with which he tried to explain all types of existing relationships, as well as the different phases they go through.

According to Sternberg, all types of couples can be classified according to three elements:

- The first of them is commitment. This is the decision made by each member of the couple to fight for their love and continue with the relationship even in bad times. It is the rational component of relationships.
- The second element that differentiates the types of relationships is intimacy. It consists of a series of feelings on the part of both members of the couple, which leads the two people to feel close and want to open up to each other. This component has to do with emotions and is responsible for creating a bond of affection between the couple, as well as a feeling of closeness.
- Finally, passion is related to a desire to unite with the other person, so that great desires (both sexual and romantic) are generated. Therefore, this component has to do mainly with sexuality.

Sternberg believed that all couples present at least one of the elements, but depending on how many and which of them are present at the same time, certain types of couples will appear. Counting on all possible combinations between passion, commitment, and intimacy, Sternberg described seven types of couples; this without counting an eighth sometimes mentioned, which is the lack of love (when there are no elements present).

For Sternberg, none of the types of love is better than another; The key—according to the researcher—is to find a person who feels the same as us to create a lasting relationship in which there is no misunderstanding.

7 Types of couples according to the triangular theory

Depending on the elements that are present within the relationship, Sternberg talked about the existence of seven possible types of relationships depending on the feeling that prevailed in them:

- **Sweetie**

These are those relationships in which the only existing component is intimacy. It is very common in friendships, but also in some relationships, it can happen. The predominant feeling is a bond and closeness with the other member of the relationship, but without a strong sexual desire or a long-term commitment.

- **Empty love**

The only component present in this type of relationship is commitment. They are usually couples who have been together for a long time, but in which both intimacy and passion have been disappearing. Although they no longer feel attracted or love each other, there is still a relationship of respect and fidelity between them. If the commitment is lost, these relationships usually end in divorce.

- **Infatuation**

It is a relationship based only on passion. Without the existence of intimacy or commitment, the two people are very attracted to each other, but they can "fall out of love" quite quickly. It is usually understood as "love at first sight."

- **Romantic love**

These are relationships that have just begun. They are formed by passion as well as intimacy, but there is still no active commitment component. Later they can acquire this element or, on the contrary, dissolve when one of the other two is finished.

- **Fatuous love**

These peculiar relationships have a commitment component, but this occurs mainly due to real passion. They would be relationships as "friends with the right to rub." In general, there is no excellent emotional bond between the people involved.

- **Sociable love**

A mixture of commitment and intimacy forms these relationships. There is no excellent sexual desire, but love is powerful. They usually occur in very long-lasting relationships, when passion dies out, or in intense friendships and relationships with family members, in which there is no romantic or sexual component.

- **Complete love**

The last type of love is formed by a mixture of intimacy, passion, and commitment. Of the seven types of couples, it is not only the most complicated to achieve but also the most difficult to maintain. In general, unless there is a conscious effort on the part of the two members of the couple, complete love usually loses some of its components and evolves towards one of the other types.

CHAPTER 9
EMOTIONAL DEPENDENCE IN ADOLESCENCE

Emotional dependence in adolescence becomes very important, on the one hand, by the nature of this dependence and, on the other, by the stage of significant development in which it occurs.

Psychology has been treating emotional difficulties such as jealousy or emotional dependence for some time. The latter presents a series of very characteristic features.

Knowing that human interactions are always complex, the society in which we live, new forms of communication, or certain personality variables, can predispose more to people having emotional dependence. If we have to address this difficulty at some stage of life, that stage is undoubtedly adolescence.

Emotional dependence in adolescence can cause much discomfort both in those who suffer and in their environment. We break down the keys to this phenomenon.

Adolescence: a stage of transition and changes

If there is one word that predominates in this vital stage, it is changing. Both from a biological point of view and from a social point of view, a series of changes take place in adolescence. Many of them affect the emotions, thoughts, and behaviors of children. We do not exaggerate by saying that at this stage, much of the personality structure develops.

However the important thing about this stage is not the changes, but how these changes occur. And that many of these, whether physical, social, emotional, or sexual ... arrive very fast. So fast, that in many situations, boys do not have the resources or maturity necessary to face many of them.

If we focus on emotional changes, it should be noted that these happen in context. That is, adolescence is a social concept since social influences mediate a lot in how boys and girls live this stage.

Emotionally, teenagers often have to endure some pressure. For example, it is quite frequent that the search for acceptance as a way of adapting to the environment makes them act in the way that best suits the group they want to belong to. Or even in relationships, there can be all kinds of pressures, and these can generate a lot of discomfort.

Relationships are a new way to bond emotionally, and not everyone has the level of self-knowledge or social skills to know how to set limits or communicate most appropriately.

Emotional dependence

Although this section is about emotional dependence in a couple, there are other emotional dependencies, such as maternal or paternal subsidiaries or in friendly relationships, without going any further. Focusing on the couple, there are many definitions of emotional dependence, but all have in common the following traits:

- **Need.** When someone has an emotional dependence, he creates a need or set of requirements. Expressly, the emotionally dependent person needs to spend time with their partner or be accepted or approved by their partner.
- **Fear.** At an intense level, the basis of emotional dependence (and also of jealousy) is usually fear. Fear of abandonment, fear of rejection or fear of loneliness are very frequent when these types of dependencies occur.
- **Reduction of freedom.** There is no emotional dependence that does not affect our freedom.

Emotional dependencies often push us to stop doing things we used to do because we liked them or to stop being with people we were comfortable with.

- **Impact on behavior, thoughts, and emotions.** The needs, discussed in the first point, affect the behavioral, cognitive and emotional levels. The perception of reality is often altered so much that those who experience situations of emotional dependence do not realize it, but the rest of their closest environment does.
- **Social isolation.** By paying more attention to the relationship and trying to devote more time, we inevitably give up spending more time with other people. Progressively, those who have an emotional dependence will want to spend more and more time with their partner and less with the rest of their social circle.

Also, it is necessary to refer to mutual emotional dependence or emotional codependency. This occurs bidirectionally by the two members of the couple and accentuates the features that define this dependence.

When an adolescent has an emotional dependence on the sphere of the couple, he should not be forced to leave it as an imposition. It is much more useful to be available to speak and, above all, to listen.

Empathy and Support are keys to dealing with people with emotional dependence. Although this situation is visible from the outside, those who experience it do not perceive it in the same way, and we must respect the times of each person.

Emotional gaps

All people have emotional differences. The important thing is to identify them, accept them and fill them in the healthiest way possible.

Surely you've heard the expression "emotional lacks" on occasion. It is a widely used expression that describes specific emotional states, which include individual attitudes and behaviors. More than talking about shortcomings, it is more accurate to speak of emotional gaps. These metaphorical gaps are common, having as a rule, more influence when they occur in childhood.

From Psychology, we use metaphors to try to describe complex phenomena. Not all metaphors are equally beneficial. Emotional gaps do form one of the metaphors that help more than hinder.

The vacuum, in this case, would not be described as a space with a pressure lower than atmospheric, as defined by Physics through the American Void Society. Instead, the meaning of this void is more in line with describing a space that tends to be filled. That is, each vacuum will generate the need to be filled by the person who has it.

After that, the emotional voids are spaces of our being that tend to be filled. And we call them emotional because their creation and their filling occur in the emotional plane. Thus, we all have our gaps, and these are changing in size according to what happens—and happened—in our lives.

Why do we have them?

Some people may think they are the product of some disorder or problem. Nothing is further from reality. Most emotional gaps arise from constant adaptation to the environment.

Life is change, and the changes that occur at the level of relationships alter our gaps, whether creating gaps, enlarging those that exist, or filling them, totally or partially, and our vital experiences condition our emotional state.

Moreover, the gaps are related to the interactions we have, not only with others, but with ourselves. Self-esteem, but especially self-concept, are keys for these gaps to affect us more or less, or we choose to fill them in a certain way.

How can they be filled?

Emotional gaps generate, in turn, the need to be "filled." It is an emotional necessity. Thus, there are many ways to fill these gaps, but mainly, they are grouped in two:

- **Fill emotional gaps through others**

The gaps can be filled with infinite elements, such as attention, acceptance, loyalty or the feeling of security.

One way to fill these 'gaps' is through the search for these elements in other people. That is, our emotional needs could be filled through the acceptance or attention of other people. But, this form is not recommended.

If we get used to filling these gaps through others, we will develop emotional dependencies in almost any relationship we have. Also, if a relationship ends, our emptiness will have to be filled again by another person or other people.

- **Fill emotional gaps through ourselves**

In a very different direction, these needs can be met through the same elements mentioned above, only here we will not look for them in other people, but in ourselves.

Thus, our gaps can be filled through our acceptance. And in this way, we will not need anyone to fill that gap, because we can fill it. Of course, this way of filling these gaps requires more time and personal work.

Utilities of this metaphor

The use of metaphors in psychology is beneficial in many areas. If we refer to this metaphor, several cases can benefit from it. This can serve as a powerful introspection tool in people who present or have presented an emotional dependence and, above all, to those who tend to give them.

Emotional gaps can be used in a more therapeutic environment as a projective tool. Indicating to the patient how he would draw or describe his emptiness, how he is, when it was last filled or when it was emptied, can help him become aware of these unconscious mechanisms that are generated in the interactions.

Emotional voids are part of our being. Rather than denying them, it should be noted how they are, how we fill them, and if there is something we can do differently so that they do not deprive us of our happiness.

CHAPTER 10
THE MEANING OF LIFE ACCORDING TO VIKTOR FRANKL

The meaning of life, according to Viktor Frankl, is to find a purpose, to assume responsibility for ourselves and other human beings. Thus, having a bright "why," we can all face the "how"; Only by feeling free and sure of the objective that motivates us, we will be able to generate changes to create a much nobler reality.

We know that there is nothing as complicated as trying to define what we call the "meaning of life. " This issue sometimes includes philosophical, transcendental and even moral nuances, which is why we very often stay in the usual old labels, namely " being happy and making others happy," "feeling satisfied," "doing good," etc.

«Man can preserve a vestige of spiritual freedom, of mental independence, even in the most terrible circumstances of psychic and physical tension.»

-Viktor Frankl-

However, many try to answer this question and experience a deep existential void. What is the meaning of life for me if all I do is work, if all my days are the same and if I don't make sense of anything around me? Faced with this common situation, the famous neurologist, psychiatrist, and founder of logotherapy, Viktor Frankl, gave a reasonably accurate response that should invite us to a proper reflection.

The human being has no obligation to define the meaning of life in universal terms. Each of us will do it our way, starting from ourselves, from our potential and experiences, discovering ourselves in our day to day lives. Moreover, the meaning of life not only differs from one person to another, but we will have a vital purpose at every stage of our existence.

The important thing is that each objective gives us satisfaction and encouragement to get up in the morning and fight for what we want.

The meaning of life for Viktor Frankl

Viktor Frankl published in 1945 "Man In Search Of Meaning," a book that inspired millions of people to assume a very firm attitude: the attitude of oneself to life. Frankl, as we know, lived in the horrors of the Holocaust by being one of the prisoners in Auschwitz and Dachau, an experience that he stoically overcame, and that allowed him to subsequently lay the foundations of a very personal type of therapy, that we know as logotherapy.

Also, something that was very clear after surviving those years and the loss of his family was that his purpose in this world was not going to be other than to help others find their sense of life, to choose their path. On the other hand, as he explained in his work, this objective was carried out starting from three particular points: work day by day with motivation, live from the sphere of love, and have the courage at all times to face adversity.

In this research conducted by the Universidad del Norte (Colombia), logotherapy, also called the Third Viennese School of Psychotherapy, is used to study a clinical case. The three basic anthropological dimensions proposed by Viktor Frankl and that make this school a way of intervention based on meaning are highlighted. The first one is the biological or somatic one, constituted by the bodily characteristics of the human being. The second, the psychic, is composed of the psychodynamic characteristics. And the third and last, the spiritual, transcends the previous ones.

Let's see below what dimensions each one of us should work on to find our own vital goals.

Live with determination

We have all seen it somewhere. There are people who, even in the most complicated circumstances, remain firm, decisive and motivated no matter how complex their reality may be. How do they do that? What material are their cells, tendons, heart or arteries made of? We all share the same biological structures, but what sets us apart from those people is their decision.

Being determined to achieve something, overcome any obstacle and fight for what we want in each moment, however small, will help us to be clear about our vital purposes at every stage of our lives.

"Everything can be taken away from man except one thing: the last of human liberties—the choice of personal attitude in a set of circumstances—to decide his path."

-Viktor Frankl-

Even if you suffer, be clear about one purpose: you will find strength.

Viktor Frankl explained in his book "Man In Search Of Meaning" that there is nothing worse than perceiving that our suffering is of no use, that pain is nothing more than the echo of hopelessness.

Now, if we can find a purpose, suffering will not only be supported, but it will become a challenge.

In this way, and before surrendering and seeing no sense in pain, we combine strengths to see in it a purpose, a vital purpose with which to feed motivation, and resistance ...

Change your attitude to find a higher sense of life

Sometimes life is not fair. Sometimes we strive to exhaustion, invest time, energy, emotions, and a piece of our own heart ... and yet, destiny brings us an unexpected setback and every effort, every dream is disintegrated. Breaking down in these cases is more than logical and understandable. Now, when this happens, we have two options.

- First, assume that we cannot change what happens to us, that we are prisoners of circumstances and that there is nothing to do.
- The second option (and the recommended one) is to accept that we cannot change what has happened to us, but we can improve our attitude towards these circumstances.

Therefore, we must be able to apply a stronger, more resilient, and positive attitude to find a more hopeful, higher sense of life.

The meaning of life does not ask, it feels

All the answers to our vital doubts are not abroad. The books will not explain to us what our sense of life is, nor will our family or friends have the right to dictate our purposes. In reality, all our existential needs, passions and objectives are within us, and what is even more interesting, will change over time as we mature, as we grow as human beings.

Thus, nothing is as essential as assuming our freedom and personal responsibility to define our goals, those that we will do even in the worst circumstances. As Viktor Frankl himself explained, each day and every moment we have the opportunity to make a decision, a decision that will determine: whether we are subject to the circumstances, as a plaything of fate, or act with true dignity, listening to our true self.

Let's think about the latter; let's work on our freedom with courage, with determination.

Existential vacuum: the feeling that life is meaningless

The existential void is a senseless spiral. A heartbreaking sensation in which the meaning of life has disappeared and only suffering and an experience of disconnection with the outside world remains.

Life has no meaning. That is the central belief of those who experience the heartbreaking sense of carelessness for living, the weight of injustices and a kind of disconnection from everything that surrounds them.

They are usually reflexive people who inquire into matters of great importance, such as death or lack of freedom, and who cannot get rid of a deep existential void that engulfs them increasingly actively. It is a void to which society contributes with its prevailing messages related to individual values and immediate satisfaction.

Although there are also those who navigate in the pursuit of pleasure with the sole purpose of anesthetizing their suffering, the difference is that the latter do not repair the emptiness they experience.

For each one, there are no answers to the reason for living. Nothing fills them; nothing satisfies them and, precisely, this ends up trapping them in a psychological state of suffering. In most cases, this situation results in deep depression or self-destructive behavior.

The existential emptiness is the spiral of nonsense, and the consequence of recognizing oneself as someone who looks at the world with a different perspective for the incongruities detected or as someone who has been carried away by the pursuit of pleasure to avoid suffering. It is a widespread phenomenon today. Let's go deeper.

In the depths of the abyss

The development of a sense of life can be frustrated when the goals and objectives are not completed or fulfilled; when the clash between expectations and reality is so intense that only disappointment makes an appearance, or when crises threaten the sense of security and certainty, and there are no adequate tools to deal with them.

All of this leads to a deep state of existential frustration that empties the person inside, and that sometimes leads them to a painful abyss. It is as if inside they house a dense desert, one in which the absurd dominates existence and almost all capacity to connect to others is lost.

For the psychologist, Benjamin Wolan, this state was called existential neurosis and defined as "the failure to find meaning in life, the feeling that one has no reason to live, to fight, to wait ... that one is unable to find a goal or a guideline in life, the feeling that, although individuals try hard in their work, they do not really have any aspiration."

Some authors, such as psychotherapist Tony Anatrella, point out the constant search to satisfy the ego is the cause of this loss of consciousness since they are selfish actions that impede the capacity for personal transcendence.

And about this, other authors affirm that the loss of meaning is associated with the disappearance of the other, the supremacy of individualistic values, and obtaining pleasure as a mechanism-erred to be happy. In this way, the person clings to their desires, and the sense of cultural references, such as coexistence, solidarity, or mutual respect among others, is diluted.

Thus, when the reality is confused and the means to achieve happiness become ends in themselves, there is a risk of falling into a vacuum. Pleasant short-term emotions, such as enjoyment or joy, provide pleasure, but not self-realization, and like all pleasure, carry the danger of creating slavery or addiction.

Somehow, man needs to do something with his life, which is not only tasty but also done by him. Therefore, the meaning of life is related to the destiny you want and need; because through that desire, man pretends to offer freedom to his development, since when he lives fully, is when his freedom transcends the limits of his immanence and understands that the meaning of his life is not reduced only to something material and finite, but to something that exceeds, goes beyond.

The problem is when this does not happen as expected, when circumstances do not meet the expectations of your life project, and nonsense takes you to the abyss of existential emptiness.

The noetic dimension of man

According to the Swiss psychiatrist Viktor Frankl, the man has mainly three dimensions:

- Physical aspect - It is conformed by the corporal scope and the biological scope.
- Psychic dimension - It is about the psychodynamic reality, that is, the psychological and emotional universe.
- Noetic dimension or spiritual dimension - It encompasses the phenomenological spheres of the soul. Therefore, this dimension transcends the other two. Also, thanks to it, the human being can integrate the painful experiences of existence and develop a healthy life on a psychological level.

Thus, when the person experiences a deep state of boredom, reluctance and is lost in the labyrinth of his existence, he has conflicts in his spiritual dimension. He is not able to integrate his wounds; he may not even identify them, neither finding a reason for its existence so that it drowns in suffering and experiences a lack of meaning, coherence, and purpose, or what is the same: an existential void.

Frankl states that this emptiness is the root of many mental disorders. That is, the break in the noetic or spiritual dimension, that feeling that existence is meaningless, is expressed in the psychological aspect through three groups of main symptoms:

- Depressive symptoms
- Aggressive traits with or without impulse control
- Addictions

In this way, people trapped in the existential void are as if with their eyes covered and their feelings with an unconscious veil, which prevents them from finding the meaning of their life, and that leads them to chronic dissatisfaction and despair. So what to do to find that sense?

In search of meaning

"Work like this, as if you lived for the second time, and the first time you had done it as misguidedly as you are about to do now."

-Viktor Frankl-

According to Swiss psychologist, Carl Jung, man needs to find meaning to continue his way in the world. Therefore, without that meaning, he is lost in nothingness, in no man's land, wandering in the labyrinth of existence.

Frankl emphasizes that values mediate the path to meaning and that social consciousness is the instrument that reveals it. Now, although the benefits arise from a personal intimacy, they end up culminating in universal values, which coincide with cultural, religious or philosophical systems.

Therefore, the connection with the other is essential so as not to lose the meaning of life, as well as the maintenance of emotional ties, as long as you do not put all the responsibility of being happy in them. Somehow, a life with meaning is a life rooted in the social.

The French sociologist and philosopher, Durkheim, reflects very well the problem of social uprooting and the consequences that it entails: [when the individual] is individualized beyond a certain point, if he separates himself too radically from other beings, men or things, he finds himself in solitary confinement with the sources that they should generally feed on, and they no longer have anything to apply to. By making the void around her, she has made the emptiness within herself, and she has nothing left to reflect more than her misery. He no longer has as an object of meditation anything other than the nothing that is in him and the sadness that is its consequence.

Now, it is not about finding the guilty or saviors, but rather adopting a reflective and responsible attitude that allows us to investigate within ourselves, find a purpose and get out of that existential void. Because there is indeed no more complicated question than what is the meaning of life for us.

It is convenient to affirm that there are multiple ways to define the meaning of life, as many as people and, even, each of us can change our vital purpose throughout our existence. Therefore, what matters, as Viktor Frankl stated, is not the meaning of life at a general level, but what meaning we give it at any given time.

Also, Frankl states that we should not inquire into the meaning of life, but understand that it is we who are concerned. That is, we can answer life by responding to our own experience. This means that responsibility is the intimate essence of our existence.

Because although we have invested time, energy, effort, and heart, life is sometimes not fair. And despite the fact that, at this moment, falling apart is entirely understandable, we have two options: to accept that we cannot change what happened, that there is nothing to do, and we are victims of the circumstances, or to allow that we cannot effectively change what has happened, but our attitude towards it.

Therefore, we are responsible for our actions, emotions, thoughts, and decisions. And consequently, we have the option of deciding why, before what, or to whom we consider ourselves responsible.

Therefore, the meaning of life is always changed; it never ceases. Every day and every moment, we have the opportunity to make decisions that will determine if we are subject to our circumstances or if we act with dignity, listening to our true self with responsibility, and free from the traps of pleasure and immediate satisfaction.

"The human being is not one more thing among other things; things determine each other, but man is ultimately his determinant. What he becomes within the limits of his faculties and his environment he has to do for himself."

-Viktor Frankl-

CHAPTER 11
PARTNER ABUSE

Partner abuse produces emotional sequelae that are not always visible to the naked eye. However, they become an obstacle for the victim since it leads to states of loneliness, anguish, and sadness.

The psychological effects of partner abuse are not always given the importance they deserve. It is sometimes thought that the only consequences of this traumatic experience are visible bumps and wounds on the body.

The truth of all is that a person who goes through this situation needs constant emotional support. Otherwise, he can be submerged in a series of negative feelings that occur as a result of the damage caused by the aggressor.

The most worrying thing is that the victim does not always know how to express it and has difficulty asking for help when he needs it. Also, he is likely to fall back into unhealthy relationships because he is accustomed to thinking that he deserves it and it is his fault.

What are the psychological effects that partner abuse can bring?

Partner abuse can be physical, psychological, or both. Regardless of this, it leaves emotional sequels that can be difficult to overcome, especially when the victim fails to externalize or accept them.

It is essential to learn to interpret their signals because they are not always quite blunt. On the other hand, they can lead to depressive states of care, since the person comes to undermine their integrity. What psychological effects are they?

- **Low self-esteem**

Low self-esteem can be a trigger and a consequence of partner abuse. When the person does not value himself, he usually falls quickly into relationships that generate emotional dependence. This makes it easier for the aggressor to deteriorate his self-esteem further.

Also, psychological abusers focus on that weakness to attack it steadily, without mercy. Therefore, the person comes to think that he is worthless and has the idea that only his victimizer can love him.

- **Anxiety and stress**

After going through an episode of violence in a relationship, the victim has a constant crisis of anxiety and post-traumatic stress. Much of this symptomatology is the manifestation of the person's denial of his situation.

On many occasions, the person who suffers is not aware of the damage caused by the aggression of their partner. When it is only psychological abuse, it may take a long time before you consider filing a complaint.

- **Loneliness**

Partner abuse can cause a tendency to loneliness and isolation in those who suffer its consequences. Because the abuser tries to cut off all of the victim's communication with his family and friends, the ability to have interpersonal relationships is later affected.

Similarly, the constant attacks on self-esteem and reputation damage prevent the person from feeling comfortable in a social environment. The worst thing is that loneliness aggravates the situation and makes it difficult to put an end to it.

- **Guilty feeling**

It is very likely that the victim, falling into a state of loneliness and low self-esteem, ends up blaming herself for what is happening to her. Also, it is not strange that the abuser applies methods of manipulation so that the person self-acts.

For example, when it comes to a case of psychological abuse, a phenomenon called "emotional blackmail" is common, in which the perpetrator uses tricks so that the other feels that their behaviors are the triggers of aggression.

- **Depression**

One of the worst psychological consequences of partner abuse is constant episodes of depression and loss of hope. Due to low self-esteem and the inability to have healthy relationships, the victim falls into depressive states.

Timely attention to this problem is significant since it can have fatal consequences. The abused person feels in a place with no exit and comes to make decisions that threaten his health or life.

- **Suicidal ideation**

Following the above problem, it is worth mentioning,

in particular, the suicidal ideation of some victims. Feeling the heartbreak of the person they loved, being involved in pain and not finding a "cure" are the reasons for wanting to stop living.

When there is no timely detection and attention to these thoughts, the outcome may be death. Therefore, before any warning sign, it is essential to seek professional psychological attention.

- **Excessive aggression**

The way to externalize the pain can be through feelings such as anger or aggression towards others. Consequently, the person feels that everyone is against him or that he cannot establish links with anyone.

To summarize, maltreatment has severe consequences for the emotional health of the victim. His lack of attention prevents an optimal recovery of leading a healthy life after overcoming the episode of violence. Therefore, it is essential to receive family support and professional care.

Boiled Frog Syndrome

The boiled frog has spent all its energy adapting to the circumstances, so when the critical moment arrives, it has no strength left to be safe.

The boiled frog syndrome refers to the emotional wear and tear that is generated when we are locked up in situations from which we believe it is impossible to escape and, therefore, we endure and endure until burned out.

Let's say that, little by little, we get into a kind of vicious circle that deteriorates us mentally and emotionally to the point of being left without strength. It was Olivier Clerc, French writer and philosopher, who raised, in a simple, accurate and illustrative language, the fable of "The boiled frog." Let's look more closely at what it consists of and how we can apply its teachings.

The boiled frog, the frog that wasted its forces

The fable is based on a real physical law that says that "if the heating rate of the water temperature is less than 0.02 °C/minute, the frog stays still and dies at the end of cooking. At a higher temperature, the frog jumps and escapes."

Thus, as explained by Olivier Clerc, if we put a frog in a bowl of water and begin to warm this little by little, the frog will gradually adjust its body temperature in parallel. When the water is reaching its boiling point, the frog can no longer regulate its temperature and, therefore, tries to jump.

Sadly, however, the frog is no longer able to do so, as it has wasted its strength in adjusting its temperature and no longer enjoys the impetus it needs to escape. As an obvious consequence, the frog dies boiled, without doing anything to jump and be saved.

Now, we must ask ourselves what killed the frog: was the water boiling, or was it unable to decide when to jump correctly?

Surely if it had been submerged in a casserole at 50 ºC, it would have made a great leap to get safe. However, while tolerating the temperature rise, it did not consider that it could and should get out of there.

This is the silent deterioration that leads us to pretend that we are well.

When the emotional decline is prolonged, it goes unnoticed to us. This justifies that we do not react, do not oppose, and that we end up drowning by breathing a toxic air that slowly poisons us. In this sense, it is common to be victims of the boiled frog syndrome in certain types of relationships, at work, in the family, with friends and even at the macrosocial level.

Thus, when dependence, pride, selfishness, or demands are manifested with droppers, we find it difficult to realize how harmful it can be to remain in that place. It may seem that we even feel pleased that our partner needs us at all times, that our boss trusts us to assign specific tasks to us or that our faithful friend continually demands our attention.

However, in the long run, the demands diminish our ability to react and respond, causing us to deplete our strength and our ability to see that it is not a healthy relationship.

Open your eyes and know yourself

The process of silent adaptation to discomfort deteriorates us and is done with the control of our lives, little by little and in a very subtle way. This prevents us from being aware and preparing to give an answer that truly fits our needs. For this reason, we must make a conscious effort to keep our eyes open. Thus, we can value what we want. Only in this way can we detract from what deteriorates our faculties.

To grow, we need to feel uncomfortable for a while and even experience bad times. During this process, you can get to know yourself better. Because getting started and enforcing our rights is something that many times those around us do not like since they live accustomed to our conformity, and for them, our attitude change is also uncomfortable.

Recall that sometimes an "Enough!" will help us guarantee our emotional well-being and safeguard our self-esteem, dignity, and interests. Let's keep the fable of the boiled frog in mind and avoid consuming ourselves in pain that can be avoided in time.

CHAPTER 12

EXERCISES THAT WILL IMPROVE YOUR RELATIONSHIP

When one is in love, happiness and passion fill the person's body and soul. Feeling real love for your partner is possible. It is possible to travel the life of the hand of a person who corresponds to that love. Now, in these cases, it is essential to take care of the person in the right way.

Sometimes, routine or carelessness causes the relationship to cool down. In love, not everything goes. It is precious to gain confidence and security over time, but it is just as important to maintain the illusion over the years.

Advancing in a relationship is not synonymous with neglect. For all this, we want to share with you five exercises to help maintain passion. To never stop taking the initiative, and continue enjoying the relationship as if it were the first day. No matter the moment you are in, it doesn't matter if you have been sharing your life for a long or short time. What matters is that you acquire the habit of doing them daily.

Keep small details: write letters

As they say, in the little details is happiness. In the relationship, affection is demonstrated every day, with real and right actions. Prepare dinner and wait for your partner to enjoy the moment. The options are numerous and are presented every minute.

For example, a beautiful detail is to write a letter to your partner. In part, it seems that the idea has been relegated to previous centuries, where it was a common way of expressing love to the loved one. But it is true that writing has many beneficial effects.

Writing allows the person to free themselves, let off steam, and capture the deepest feelings on paper. In your letter, you can expose what you feel for your partner and confess your feelings.

You probably think that your partner already knows what you feel for her, but this is one of the big mistakes we fall into. Yes, in the relationship, the other person usually knows, but it never hurts to be reminded. Do it with a letter, put effort, get excited while you write. These will be symptoms that you are doing well.

Samples of love: hug each other every day

When we have been with our partner for a few years, the signs of affection sometimes tend to decrease. Some couples are even reluctant to be affectionate in public; they are ashamed.

Interestingly, this does not happen so much at the beginning of the relationship. And it should in no case decrease. Life is short enough to go around with nonsense, specifically, when we are talking about love. Those who can hug their better half should be considered lucky, so they should never stop doing so—less for shame.

Therefore, the habit of hugging each other in the relationship is an exercise that you should not do without any day of your life. A hug will bring you closer, unite you and allow you to show how much you love each other.

Relationship: make love without hurrying

Making love is a pleasant activity that we should always enjoy calmly. It is an intimate act of trust, in which you can demonstrate without taboo how much you feel for the other.

However, obligations, work, and schedules can sometimes make it difficult to find an auspicious moment to devote to sex. Although it costs, it is essential to take some time to dedicate and enjoy it thoroughly.

If we make love in a hurry, we can fall into a terrible routine or forget about it because it is no longer pleasant. There is still much to know about our bodies. Do not allow sex to become a mechanical act. Enjoy it.

A relationship does not maintain itself; it needs care, pampering, people who are genuinely involved in it. If all this does not exist, perhaps a day will come when everything will collapse. It is possible to make all dreams come true from the hand of those who love each other. It is not so challenging to enjoy love.

Habits That Help You Improve Your Sex Life

Did you know that among the many benefits that physical exercise brings us is improving libido and achieving a fuller sexual life?

Having an active sex life is one of the aspects that influences mood, emotional health, and physical well-being. For this reason, it is essential that we pay attention to this aspect of our life and not underestimate it.

Although we associate sexual relations with pleasure and reproduction, its benefits go beyond all this. They could compromise the functions of several major body systems. Do you want to know more about this? Throughout this chapter, we will reveal some benefits that, possibly, we did not know before.

Sex is one of the essential pillars of relationships, not only because it strengthens emotional relationships, but because it improves communication and trust. However, sometimes, libido may decrease and, since it reduces sexual performance or fullness is not reached, inconveniences begin to arise.

For this reason, it is essential to lead a healthy lifestyle. Next, we share with you the six main habits to notice an improvement in your sex life. We encourage you to test them because you will begin to see the difference.

1. Have a healthy diet

Although most people ignore it, good eating habits influence both libido and sexual performance. While a fat-based and processed diet can affect the activity of sex hormones, organic foods help improve it.

These are a significant source of energy and essential nutrients that, in addition to improving fitness, keep hormones in balance. It should also be noted that there are some foods with aphrodisiac properties, which, when ingested regularly, can increase sexual desire. Be sure to increase the consumption of:

- Fresh fruits and vegetables.
- Whole grains.
- Grains and legumes.
- Lean meats
- Blue Fish.

2. Manage stress

Stress is one of the main enemies of sexual life for both men and women. Overwork, partner discussions, and economic problems can increase this mood, which, in turn, decreases sexual desire.

Its lack of control increases the feeling of physical fatigue and, although we do not notice it, stress also influences the uncontrol of some hormones. Because of this, it is essential to handle it promptly, putting into practice relaxation therapies, resting, and performing pleasant activities.

3. Exercise

All those who are going through a crisis should take into account the multiple benefits of physical activity for the sexual field. Exercise improves many aspects of physical health, increases the production of wellness hormones, and, with this, improves libido.

Daily exercise balances hormones such as serotonin and endorphins, both associated with pleasant sexual intercourse. Also, it strengthens the muscles of the whole body. Thus, by improving physical performance, it helps to achieve more lasting sexual intercourse.

Those activities focused on strengthening the pelvic floor could help in cases of sexual dysfunctions such as vaginismus and anorgasmia. Some of the exercises we can perform are known as Kegel and, many times, are recommended by doctors.

4. Avoid tobacco

A large number of cases of people with problems in their sexual life are related to their addiction to smoking. Sexual dysfunctions, as well as decreased libido, can be caused by the effects of the toxins contained in the cigarette.

These substances compromise the activity of sex hormones and, since they affect circulation, also intervene in the functioning of the reproductive organs. Therefore, it is essential to reduce this type of harmful habits in our lives.

5. Avoid toxic relationships

The emotional level is a fundamental pillar in the sexual field and, therefore, having a toxic relationship can prevent reaching fullness. In relationships, it is necessary to feel trust, complicity, and mutual love. These are components that lead to a better understanding of sexual intercourse.

Those who are victims of pressure, blackmail, or violence by their partner do not enjoy the sexual act and, in some way, do so in a mandatory manner. Therefore, it is essential to identify these behaviors. Their lack of control can generate physical and emotional impacts on the victim.

6. Improve sexual information

Sex education is essential to improve sex life in all aspects. Not only does it allow us to know how to improve the sexual act as such, but it also helps to promote the self-knowledge of our bodies and the elements that are required to achieve fullness.

Of course, in addition to the cited habits, there are many other influential sexual habits that should be considered when something is not going well. Having excellent communication with your partner and getting out of the routine are other additional components that also help to improve sex life. Keep these recommendations in mind and, if you need it, ask for professional help.

CHAPTER 13
LOVE, A CONSCIOUS CHOICE

In order not to beg for love and not cling to the first person that appears, we must first learn to love ourselves and be alone. It is the only way not to create a dependent relationship.

Love is something significant to us. We are looking for that person with whom to share our life, with which to live incredible experiences and moments.

However, have you ever wondered if that love has been a conscious choice? Why do you always end up encountering the same profile of a person you don't like?

Perhaps all this has its raison d'être in the fact that you do not consciously choose who to maintain a relationship with, but it is the others who choose you.

Low self-esteem in love

Low self-esteem and love don't get along very well. Why? Because many times we don't start dating someone because we want to, but out of necessity.

The fear of loneliness, of being unable to hold ourselves responsible for our lives, of leaving our happiness in the hands of other people, causes us not to choose who to go out with but instead they choose us. For that reason, when we ask ourselves why we always end up with people who do not value us, who mistreat us or who, sooner or later, make us suffer, the answer lies in us.

We are the ones who cause ourselves to always fall in the same networks, and this is a conscious choice. Sometimes, even the grip of emotional dependence catches us due to the low self-esteem that we cannot raise.

Love, then, becomes a lifesaver, and when it falters, we begin to get very nervous. However, if you have ever experienced this, you will know that you end up not being happy and living in unsatisfactory relationships. All this will make your self-esteem look even more depleted.

The rush of rushing

Being alone is not well seen. If you have ever been without a partner, you will have discovered yourself observing others who are in relationships and wishing you were, someday, in that situation. Also, we believe that the older we are, the lower the chances of having a partner. Therefore, we end up rushing, so as not to be left alone.

However, all this causes us not to know ourselves, so that we don't know what we want from the other person and end up in disastrous love relationships.

Why are there so many divorces? Why can a person have many partners, and yet none of them work? Maybe because he can't wait.

Pressure from the society where family and friends always ask us, "don't you have a partner yet?" does not help us at all not to rush into choosing that person we are not entirely sure of. It seems that having a partner is everything. Without this, we consider ourselves unsuccessful. It doesn't matter if we are not the perfect match. We settle for being with someone, anyone.

Your life project

What happens when we dive into a relationship? Suddenly, we do not think of friends, we leave what we were passionate about, and we begin to focus too much on the other person. Without realizing it, we end up not being ourselves.

This happens when we are so worried about finding a partner that we do not choose consciously; we let others do it, and we give our body and soul to the relationship.

However, we forget that a relationship is not based on sharing the same path but that each member walks in different ways but which go in the same direction.

Leaving our identity aside will be charged very expensive in the future. Our self-esteem will be trampled, and we will invest time and energy in a relationship that is predestined for failure.

Choose your partners consciously. Discover what you want and what your insurmountable limits are. Doing this will prevent you from undermining your self-esteem and being unhappy.

Do not rush. You don't have to have a partner. Cultivate yourself, take care of yourself, and don't expect anyone to do it for you. Love yourself before loving another person, and, only by doing this, when the time comes, you will know for sure who you want to have by your side.

The balm of emotional dependence

Although it may cost us, and we may experience relapses, zero contact with the person subject to our dependence will be beneficial to overcome them and begin to put ourselves first.

Emotional dependence causes us to tie ourselves to a relationship for fear of being alone or not finding anyone else.

Therefore, having zero contact in these circumstances is more than recommended.

Sometimes, this type of emotional dependence causes us to choose partners that can harm us.

There may be cases of psychological or physical abuse, manipulations, lies, infidelities ...

However, that may not be so.

What does have to be clear is that any relationship based on an emotional dependence on the other is toxic.

Emotional dependence or "I can't live without you."

The fear of being alone can cause us to believe that we cannot live without the other person.

However, in reality, it is not so.

If the other person leaves us and there is no possibility of returning , then, what do we do? We enter a new relationship immediately.

People who are afraid of being alone and who depend on others do so because they believe that only then they can be happy.

Their self-esteem is so low that their life and personality are that of the person they are attached to.

Therefore, when a break occurs, they feel empty. They haven't taken care of themselves; they don't know what they like or what their dreams are. They are lost.

The reason they are so tied to someone is not that they believe it is for a lifetime or that they cannot live without that person. They can't live without any person!

Therefore, it is normal for them to accumulate one relationship after another. All of them fail, but they don't know why.

The reason is that they choose their partner based on a need, not because they feel real love.

The importance of zero contact in an emotional dependent

When a psychologist recommends that a person has to implement zero contact with the person he depends on, this seems impossible.

Thinking about blocking him from WhatsApp, not answering his calls, or saying "no" if he gets in touch with her to stay looks like something she can never make happen.

Sometimes, she feels very guilty, because she falls into his trap, and then feels terrible. The type of dependent relationship she maintains does not make her happy, and she knows it.

A person with dependency has moments of clarity in which she says, "I have to go," "I would be better off alone than with this person," "He doesn't make me feel good."

However, this force that can invade the dependent at certain times and that points them in the right way can also, in other circumstances, lead them the wrong way.

Patience, willpower and time

Getting out of emotional dependence even by implementing zero contact is not something that happens overnight.

As with any other addiction, time and patience are needed, as there will be relapses.

The zero contact will be thrown down, but we will have advanced one step.

We become more aware, and more often we realize that we are not well if we continue like this.

This is very important.

All emotional dependents stumble over and over again on the same stone.

They do it until they make those moments of lucidity more and more present.

When the time comes, after a period of time fighting against their demons, they manage to open their eyes completely and make a decision that will undoubtedly benefit them.

You can get out of emotional dependence.

We can shake off the beliefs that tell us that without a partner, we are unhappy.

Once we have one foot out of the tendency to enter into addictive relationships, we can begin to love, honor, and respect each other.

Thus we will establish healthy relationships in which we will not depend on or need others.

Five masked control mechanisms

In the relations between parents and children and in romantic relationships, sometimes masked control mechanisms are established. They are means to put one person at the service of the other, without this becoming fully apparent.

Masked control mechanisms are strategies that some people employ to manipulate the behavior of others. Their objective is to exercise power and dominion. Therefore, they are an attack on autonomy.

Sometimes these control attempts are very obvious. It occurs when the tax behaviors are direct and leave no doubt. For example, with arbitrary mandates, intimate shouts or overt pressures. However, other times, what is implemented are control mechanisms that can go unnoticed for those who are victims of them.

" The attempts to overcome this duality, to tame the wayward and tame what has no brake, to make the unknowable foreseeable and to chain the wandering are the death sentence of love ."

-Zygmunt Bauman-

These types of masked control mechanisms are very harmful since they are not easily identifiable. They entangle people in a very confusing knot, in which they can remain for a long time without being aware of what is happening. That is why it is worth mentioning them with their names. These are five of them.

1. Control by fault

It is one of the most common and also the most harmful. It has to do with generating lines of thought or ideas that lead someone to feel guilty, without any reason for it. They take place in all kinds of relationships, but they are especially prevalent in the bond between parents and children or in the couple.

The most typical example is the one who says, "Look at everything I've done for you. " Those who say this keep a detailed account of all the acts carried out for the benefit of the other. And they charge them one by one. They self-victimize to make the other feel guilty. Many times they succeed, and with that, they maintain control over others.

2. Codependency, one of the masked control mechanisms

This is one of the masked control mechanisms that is often confused with deep affection. The keyword here is "need." It corresponds to all those expressions and behaviors in which the other is made to feel that he is indispensable to do or not do something. Even to live. "I cannot live without you."

At the same time, this type of mechanism also includes the opposite message: "You need me." In this way, a whole series of behaviors are developed to prevent the other from doing what he is capable of doing. You are given aids or supports that you have not requested and the idea that you need the one who provides that constant support is being strengthened.

3. Retention of love

This masked control mechanism is based on the manipulation of affections. Respect is given to the other when he does exactly what his manipulator wants him to do. At the same time, it is removed when he departs from the mandates or requirements of those who intend to control him.

In that sense, it is effective blackmail that, however, is not always so obvious. Many times obedience is demanded to argue that it is for the sake of the one who "must" obey. Or it is pointed out that this giving and removing of affections is a way of putting healthy limits on things.

4. Common goal

This also occurs frequently between parents and children or with couples. One of the parties "sells" one of its goals to the other. Thus, an individual goal subtly becomes a goal of two, although one of the parties is not entirely convinced that it is what they want.

That common goal sometimes becomes a sword of Damocles. The promoter of the same will have no problem expressing his "disappointment" if the other does not fit that goal, or does not do whatever it takes to obtain it. The matter may be related to a commercial purpose, to have children, or to realize specific dreams.

5. Emotional incest

While referring to abuse, this is one of the masked control mechanisms that fundamentally affects the family. In particular, it is a type of control that appears between mothers and daughters, or between fathers and daughters. The father, or the controlling figure, make the son feel that he is all for him. And that together they form a kind of "front against the world."

In the end, daughters or sons end up being a kind of parents to their parents: those who support and guide them. Also, they are the ones who often assume responsibilities that would correspond to them. They learn to give a lot without expecting anything and have a hard time understanding the sense of individuality.

All these masked control mechanisms are filtered daily in our human relationships. They are born of insecurity or frustration and lead to the same thing: uncertainty and frustration. Neither the one who implements them, nor the one who is a victim of them achieve a fulfilled and happy existence.

CHAPTER 14
THE RELIEF OF LETTING GO OF CONTROL

Between maintaining control and being a controller, there is an ocean of difference. Our survival instinct requires us to seek to keep situations under control because we do not usually tolerate uncertainty well. We do not know what will happen or if we can deal with the consequences of something that generates too much despair, especially on some occasions ...

Some people do not settle for this. They want to be decisive in all situations: indicate the direction, decide the route to follow, and say the last word. And not only when they are present, but also at a distance (to "remote control"). Those people are the controllers.

Controller features

The person who chooses to be a controller suffers a huge emotional expense. One of its most notorious features is a constant concern. However, this concern rarely becomes a planned action to resolve the reason for the anguish. Theirs is slightly stressed without acting. They waste a lot of time trying to convince others to be like them.

A controller is also an irritable person. They carry a lot of anxiety within themselves, and sometimes the smallest problems aggravate it. It is mainly obfuscating that someone opposes them, that another thinks or acts in a different sense than they would. They do not respect visions or realities different from theirs.

They also tend to have a catastrophic view of life. They see the dangers and negative consequences everywhere. That reinforces their controlling position, supposedly because they try to avoid greater evils. Deep down, the controller is a deeply insecure person. Fears have taken hold of him, and he often has strong feelings of inferiority. He compensates them like this: trying to control everything.

They are also usually invaded with guilt and have a hard time enjoying life. They hardly laugh and rarely act spontaneously. It is not uncommon to see them sad and depressed because they also have a low tolerance for frustration.

How to free yourself?

The controller lives in a jail that he has built. He cannot stop being as he is, by merely proposing it. This is because there are many fears inside that he may not have recognized, or against which he feels too vulnerable.

The first thing is: identify the sources of fear. Finally, what is the threat? How real are those dangers over which you should have the most control? Do you defend yourself from the environment, or is it possible that you are protecting yourself from your destructive impulses towards others?

Sooner or later, a controlling person also becomes irritating to others. His attitude generates rejection because no one good likes to have a watchman, supposedly smarty, next door. At that point, the controller has no choice but to isolate himself or make use of aggression to subdue others. In that kind of situation, nobody leaves well at the end.

The life of the controller is sad. And the best thing you can do for yourself is to try to do completely free activities: that do not have a definite objective, do not imply competition with others, or put into play high costs. We are talking about recreational or artistic activities, which have value on their own and do not go after a useful purpose.

If you are on that strip of people, fight to free yourself. Perhaps losing control is the only way to gain fullness. The first step is to accept it, to know that you have these characteristics, to initiate the change later, since what we deny submits to us, but what we accept can transform us ...

- **Acceptance**

The acceptance process and the need for control are in conflict most of the time they meet. "Why do I have to accept it?" "I don't like it that way." ... These are issues and complaints that we hear very often. Accepting is not synonymous with being passive to what happens. As some say, erroneously: "To accept is to swallow and resign yourself with what happens." Accepting is not "swallowing" or resigning with what happens in our day to day lives.

When something happens that we dislike, accepting it consists of observing the fact itself and the emotion that it unleashes in us. Observe, without getting involved, without clinging to the anger that it may cause us. Analyzing the situation can make us understand that we have no control over everything. In this way, instead of protesting and suffering every time something happens that we do not like, we will be aware that life is not made in our image and likeness.

Our ego tells us that everything must be a concrete form, but our ego does not matter to life. Life takes its course regardless of our tastes. So the best way to start the acceptance process is to know that trying to adapt life to us will always bring us problems because everything changes. Thus, it is healthier to learn to adapt ourselves to the possible changes in life.

Useless perfectionism

The secret to living happily has to do with finding balance points in everything we do. Perfectionism is one of those attributes in which there is significant ambiguity. It is a unique and highly valued in the professional world, but, at the same time, it causes more problems than benefits in the emotional realm.

Perfectionism is present in people with obsessive traits. Perfectionism is a desire, never filled, to reach a result that does not generate even the slightest questioning.

In that sense, it is an impossible desire, in which excellence is generally sought, and there is little tolerance for frustration. Thus perfectionist people, if they don't know how to find the midpoint of their willingness to perfection, can experience continuous discomfort.

The relationship between perfectionism and anguish

Whoever decides to use perfectionism as their primary criteria for acting, is at risk of paying a price that is too high for it. Along with the eagerness to do everything without blemish, episodes of anguish, permanent tension, and fear often also appear.

The perfectionist has a hard time enjoying his achievements. As he focuses his gaze towards that end that could be loose or that little black dot on the white sheet, the results will never seem meritorious. Not even enough. To the perfectionist, the search for the perfect leads to permanent frustration since getting everything perfect is impossible.

In many cases, perfectionism is associated with problems of low self-esteem. It may have been installed in one's life because the education that was received was very severe and placed greater emphasis on failures than on successes. That is why the idea that we are not good enough is forged; that nothing we do is measurable. Perfectionism, then, operates as a compensation mechanism for the poor image we have of ourselves.

What distinguishes an applied and committed person from someone obsessed with perfectionism, is the degree of satisfaction that he manages to experiment with what he does. One who feels pride in their work and wants to do it well will be happy to conclude a job well done, even knowing that it is not 100% perfect. The obsessive person does not experience gratification for his work, but a hint of anguish for everything he failed to do.

Myths and realities about perfectionism

There are several myths about perfectionism. They are misconceptions that conceal the true nature of this obsessive attitude. For example, some think that if they do not stay in a perfectionist line, then they will fall into neglect and mediocrity. As if there were only two extremes: perfection or carelessness. They forget that there are many intermediate points and that we are human, not infallible machines.

Another widespread myth says that only those who set out to make everything perfect achieve significant success. This is not true either. Success depends on talent and perseverance. It is much better to succeed as a relaxed person who does not have to deal with heavy doses of anguish and tension. There are many examples in the world of people who achieve high goals, without constantly evaluating what was missing or what was leftover in everything they do.

What is certain is that perfectionists rely heavily on their own and others' approval, based on too strict morals. They tend to make slightly negative criticisms and fear rejection. Also, they think that error and failure are synonyms; they have not learned to take advantage of mistakes.

The reality is that successes or failures are not what defines our value as people. If you are one of those people who do not tolerate imperfections, it may be time for you to check who you are and how much you are worth.

Freeing ourselves from perfectionism means living without being under pressure, being more emotionally responsible for ourselves, and more flexible.

CHAPTER 15
HOW TO WORK ASSERTIVE COMMUNICATION IN THE COUPLE?

Communication is the basis of any relationship, and assertiveness is a fundamental element in it. Now, how can you work, and what role do you play in your relationship?

Among all the communicative styles that exist, assertiveness is one of the most effective. However, few people can put it into practice, especially in their emotional relationships. For this reason, today, we will discover how to work assertive communication in a relationship even before conflicts appear.

Assertiveness: definitions and dimensions explain that this social ability is a "behavior that expresses the feelings and thoughts of an individual honestly without hurting those of others." As we see, this is essential in every relationship, so it is necessary to work assertive communication in the relationship.

Ways to work assertive communication in the couple

Assertive communication in the couple can be practiced every day with small passion. Simple actions. But, so that they take effect, and that when a discussion is experienced, the members of the relationship get reinforced instead of injured, it is recommended to incorporate them into the routine.

Express what we think and feel

It may seem obvious, however, in some relationships, the thoughts or feelings they harbor are rarely expressed. For example, if it bothers us that the other person plays music very loud, instead of telling them, we may prefer to shut up to avoid conflict.

This is counterproductive since we can end up exploding. Also, these uncomfortable moments that we can experience in our day are an opportunity to work assertive communication in the relationship. It is better not to shut up and, with respect, ask the other person to turn down the music.

Learn to speak for ourselves

For some reason, we don't usually talk in the first person when we argue with someone. Thus, we blame our partner with great ease and may even throw phrases like "because my friend also sees things like I do," for example.

This is a mistake since it does not allow us to work assertive communication in the relationship. Learning to speak in the first person helps us take responsibility for our emotions and verbalize them. If we don't know how to do it, we can use the phrases "I feel ..." or "I have perceived ...".

"We have two ears and one mouth to hear twice what we speak."

-Epictetus-

Before attacking, better ask

How many times have we attacked our partner if they has told us, "You are very messy" or "I don't like you doing this like this"? Our reaction is usually aggressive rather than assertive. If we were already accustomed to being assertive instead of attacking, we would ask.

For example, if our partner tells us that we are very messy, we can ask him how we can improve this or why he thinks feels this way. Hence, we will initiate a dialogue that will lead us to an attractive solution for both parties. Because, sometimes, it seems as if our partner is our enemy and that is not so.

Think before speaking

Although there are many other ways of working on communication in the couple, all of them, as we mentioned, must be practiced every day. Of course, some tips can be of great help when we start a discussion to avoid falling into old patterns of behavior:

- *Thinking about the message, but also the ways:* feeling hurt or even attacked, can cause us to harm our partner. For this reason, it is better to breathe, keep calm, and think before speaking. No hurry. Not thinking before speaking can invalidate your message and generate a real conflict.
- *Let's empathize with our partner:* learn to put yourself in the place of the other person, something precious if you know them well.
- *Do not accumulate complaints:* as we mentioned, it is preferable to express what bothers you when you feel it ... and not in a conversation about something else.

«*Effective communication begins with listening.*»

-Robert Gately-

Let's take advantage of all the moments of our day to work assertive communication in the relationship. Thus, little by little, we will build an intimacy in which trust grows.

Remember that hurting ourselves through words is not constructive, but rather, destructive. As Satir says,

The couple's bond: an affective possibility of growing up. Let's not forget to express ourselves in a "direct, honest and respectful way."

Intolerance to frustration in relationships

When our partner lives in continuous failure for what we do or say, we face prejudice (although we dare not call it that). Moreover, this low resistance to failure is an evident emotional immaturity that can often lead to psychological abuse.

Intolerance to frustration in relationships is one of the great workhorses. Some people do not accept specific reactions, decisions, or behaviors of the other and demand a change. When this does not happen, anger and frustration arise because when there is no tolerance or acceptance, it results in these problematic behaviors.

This reality is not new. The low tolerance for frustration is one of the most common emotions and, in turn, the worst managed by humans. Something that we should have overcome already in childhood crawls into adult life. It is loaded like that core matter of life that we never examined again. And the ravages it causes can be immense.

Therefore, it is easy to reach a relationship with that bomb embedded inside us, the one that, at the minimum, explodes. It does when we encounter some opposition or when some things are not as we want and expect. Then, we demand that those realities that do not please change, like the child who does not want to eat vegetables and asks for dessert directly.

The situations that can be created when someone does not know how to handle their frustration have little comics. It generates discussions, discomforts, distances, and an immense emotional impact. While it is true that we should all reach the heart of a loving relationship with the issue of frustration already overcome, that is one of the most recurring problems today.

Intolerance to frustration in relationships, how does it appear?

A person who knows how to handle frustration lives with less stress. Also, he has a better awareness of his emotions and knows how to channel them, calm them, and use them in his favor. Achieving this personal craft requires time, but once it is made, not only does life change, but we also perceive clear improvements in our dealings with people.

Now, as we have pointed out, the zero effectiveness in handling this dimension appears with increasing frequency. Thus, something that we should take into account is the fact that they point to us from studies such as those carried out by Dr. John Dollar, from the University of London (United Kingdom). In this work, published in 2013, the precise relationship between low tolerance for frustration and aggressive behavior was noted.

With aggressive behavior, there is no exclusive reference to possible physical violence. The most common is the psychological one, where words and attitudes restrict the rights of the other. In this way, intolerance to frustration in relationships often leads to the latter type of abuse. Let's see how it appears.

My wishes are my needs ... and I want them now

The person with low frustration confuses desires with needs; what he wants at any given time, he wants it now. If he does not obtain it, he projects the blame on the other person, often with wicked humor.

Moreover, sometimes, they resort to silence or the law of ice, where they ignore each other for a while. These are child behaviors executed in adults that bring as we can imagine, serious consequences.

Emotional explosions, what I feel controls me, and I project it on you

Another characteristic of frustration intolerance in relationships is the inability to handle emotions. In this way, the person who does not know how to handle this reality lives continuously harassed by his anger. Far from recognizing his inability to control his emotions, he limits himself to blaming the other for his discomfort.

If you don't do what I want, I leave you

When the person dominated by frustration does not get what he wants, he threatens to break up. For relationships that continuously deal with this problem, it is common that one partner has left several times and restarted their relationship with others. It is a vicious circle of wear and blackmail, blame projection, reproach, and constant suffering.

I live with a person who doesn't know how to handle frustration, what can I do?

Life with a person who is eternally frustrated has the taste of unhappiness. We are facing an immature personality and, someone with this profile will not only shape immature behaviors but will often result in passive-aggressive behaviors. Blackmail, victimhood, emotional manipulation, reproach, and constant anger will appear ...

One who gets frustrated and accumulates anger, because they are not as expected, does not understand acceptance and tolerance. The best thing in these cases is not to give in to the demands of those who want to control us to calm their frustration. What needs to be done is to set limits, and explain why it is not possible to give in at all. A relationship is knowing how to work as a team, not living in an emotional dictatorship.

If we do not see changes or improvements, we must make a decision. Because it is not our task to re-educate the other, to be a partner is not to be a father or a mother. Once you reach adulthood, everyone must be aware of their shortcomings and work on them, and a priority on our path to maturity is precisely knowing how to tolerate frustration.

CHAPTER 16
THE CONSEQUENCES OF ALCOHOLISM IN THE RELATIONSHIP

When alcoholism is present in the relationship, it can be thought that both have serious problems. The most common is that both find difficulties with their autonomy and that they use each other so as not to face the fact that they are responsible for themselves.

Alcoholism in the relationship is a very erosive factor for the bond, and even for the family in general. This situation sometimes creates very complex pictures in which rejection and violence are mixed with feelings of dependence and guilt. Whenever one of the two has this disease, both end up participating in it in one way or another.

If there is alcoholism in the relationship, there is also a dilemma that torments and is rarely resolved. The non-alcoholic spouse will always be in a dilemma between helping a person who needs help or leaving him to his fate to solve his problem. In this framework, a bond that is very difficult to break is often forged, since it is based on mutual dependence.

Alcohol is a powerful drug, which destroys health and ends up completely changing the way of thinking and behavior of a person. As the addiction progresses, the values, meaning of life, and ability to communicate with oneself and with others deteriorate severely. Therefore, alcoholism in the relationship is often devastating.

" Love is like wine, and like wine too, some comfort and others destroy."

-Stefan Zweig-

Some notes on alcoholism

Surely we have all heard it said, but it is never enough to remember it once again: addiction is a disease. It is not merely a habit, nor a passing episode that is lived when bad times come. Usually, it is installed slowly and gradually in a person's life.

The fact that alcohol is a socially accepted drug helps its development. Many call it "social lubricant." The spaces and occasions that have alcohol as a central guest are very varied. Therefore, the notion of reasonable consumption is easily lost.

If a person has many social activities, it is not surprising that he drinks frequently, but that does not generate any apprehension in those around him. What defines the alcoholic are two traits:

- Once he drinks the first cup, he finds it impossible to stop until he is seriously drunk ;
- When you drink, your way of being changes dramatically.

Alcoholism in the relationship

The predisposition to addictions is a reality that includes physical and psychological aspects. From the physical point of view, there are often genetic or functional circumstances that predispose to chemical dependence. From the psychological point of view, there is also a personality type or a mental picture that inclines to the development of addiction.

The most common is that a potentially alcoholic or drug-dependent person seeks as a partner someone who also has dependency traits. If he is a man, he will look for a woman with markedly maternal features. If she is a woman, she will look for a man of a protective type, between fatherly and motherly.

In this way, a whole structure is installed that makes the existence and permanence of addiction possible. Alcoholism ends up becoming a factor that separates, but also one that unites.

Once alcohol is found to be causing problems, the non-alcoholic spouse is likely to try to protect, or overprotect, their partner. They need each other.

The deterioration of the relationship

When alcoholism is present in the relationship, the most common is that in the beginning, the husband or wife becomes a kind of accomplice of the other. They will justify to others when their partner has drunk too much, or they will lie so that they do not have problems at work. It is also possible that they even help you get alcohol. That establishes codependency.

However, abusive alcohol consumption, sooner rather than later, ends up having a series of effects on the relationship. The affected person loses their sexual desire or fails to have regular sexual performance. Their altered nervous system prevents it. Likewise, alcohol leads to progressive isolation.

Nevertheless, the most destructive is the fact that alcoholism usually activates aggressive or violent reactions. In many cases, this leads to situations where there are different forms of violence, including psychological. Generally, it is then the partner begins to feel overwhelmed by the situation.

This should lead to the breakdown of the relationship. However, frequently, that does not happen. The bond persists and is filled with hatred, resentment, and compassion at the same time, both on one side and the other.

The codependent, with his actions, prevents the other from assuming his problem and making decisions. The clerk uses the other as a means of not sinking completely. It is a dramatic situation that requires professional help.

CHAPTER 17
THE PLASTICINE SYNDROME

The plasticine person syndrome causes someone to devote their attention to the care of others, leaving aside their well-being. This curious phenomenon affects not only the morale of the person in question but also those who care about them.

By taking care of the needs of others, they leave their well-being in the background. Not only are they concerned with meeting the needs of others but also based on practice, they acquire a unique ability to intuit them. So the center of their attention is always pointing towards the people around them.

The person who has the plasticine syndrome gives himself so much to others that he ends up forgetting himself.

Features that characterize a plasticine person

In relationships with others, worrying about their concerns and problems, is an excellent way to care for and strengthen our relationships. But, beware, like any right attitude, when taken to the extreme, it can cause significant damage to the person who sustains it. Next, we show you some of the features that best characterize the plasticine person:

1. They forget their desires and needs

"Plasticine people" are those who give themselves so much to others that they forget their individual needs and concerns, relegating to the background any desire other than to benefit others. This can significantly wear down the person who supports this attitude: it is tough, if not impossible, for someone to cover their own needs for which they do not care.

2. Do not expect to receive anything from others

This syndrome has a sturdy anchor that supports it: we talk about a way of acting that can count on many positive reinforcements at the social level. Also, we talk about people who give without waiting/accepting anything in return.

This lack of demand or request differentiates them from toxic people, who use their offerings and concessions as a form of manipulation to get what they want from others. They only do favors when they need something from the other, unlike the plasticine person.

Plasticine people expect nothing in return, unlike toxic people.

3. They are very generous people

A plasticine person tends to confuse generosity with neglecting himself. Although being generous is positive, their extreme dedication makes them very vulnerable to manipulative people who are willing to use their excessive delivery for their interests.

4. They are excessively servile people

Individuals who suffer from this plasticine syndrome often become instruments for others. Also, they may feel bad when they look around and do not find an alien need to cover. It is in these moments when they feel lost or of little value. Let us think that their self-esteem is very conditioned by the degree of help they can provide.

One of the causes of the discomfort of plasticine people is not finding a need of others to cover.

How to overcome plasticine syndrome

To increase your self-esteem and start prioritizing your needs, you can follow some simple strategies:

- If they ask you for a favor, think about the answer. Reflect on what it means for you to meet that person and value the cost of acquiring an absolute commitment.

- If you want to say no, do it. This is the most difficult, but if you are healthy and confident, and you explain your reasons reasonably, no one has to bother with your decision.
- Leave the guilt aside. Although guilt approaches you when you refuse to do something for another person, know that this is the best for you, since you also have your own needs.
- If you identify with any of the features that we have described in the previous section, remember that you have desires and needs that only you can attend. Either because others do not realize or because they cannot, there is a part, essential in the long run for your emotional balance, that only you can satisfy. In the end, the person's plasticine syndrome is still an indirect form of dependence.

CONCLUSION
TO LOOK FOR LOVE IS TO FIND YOURSELF

Many women yearn for love in their lives but ignore that finding love involves loving themselves first. Searching for love means finding oneself first. About this idea, a good part of the book, "Hunger of Love," by Ana Moreno (Obelisco, 2016), and some related purposes, we will cover in the following lines.

From woman to woman, I ask you: why do you need to have a partner to complete a part that you feel is missing, to fill an inner void, because you are afraid of being alone? Why do you feel helpless alone? If you have not discovered it, I am going to tell you one thing: having a partner will not solve any of these problems, that is, if it does not make them worse.

To propose such a relationship, from co-dependence, only leads to sentimental failure. Only from a conscious relationship is it possible to have a healthy couple life.

«Relationships are not meant to make us happy but conscious.»

-Raimon Samsó-

True love is born within you

Women need to feel loved. But true love is born within ourselves. A woman who loves herself radiates love and gets love. You can't attract something you don't have into your life.

«The real way to find love is to know ourselves made of love and decide to share it without expectations with the whole world.»

-Ana Moreno-

If you do not feel that you are loved, you will believe that you need another to complete you, but in that need to complete yourself, you will try to possess the other, because, without him, you feel that you are nothing. But this is a selfish way of acting. And love and selfishness are not compatible concepts.

Something even more important is to keep in mind that, just as you cannot attract love if you do not have love, what you will attract is the same as what you have to offer. If you strive to look like who you are not, you will not find an authentic person. If you do not show genuine love and respect for yourself, you will find someone who not only does not love or respect himself but will not love and respect you either.

«Searching for love does not consist in finding another person, but in finding yourself, because you are love. When you accept that you already have love in you, then you will manifest love in your life. Of the same quality and with the same intensity as the one you have for yourself.»

-Ana Moreno-

It is never too late to discover

Whether you have not yet found a partner, or you are not satisfied with the relationship you have, it is never too late to find yourself, to start cultivating it from the inside, instead of seeking love. For Ana Moreno, it is as simple as acting with respect, with honesty and appreciation, sharing with others, giving to others.

The great thing about this way of understanding love is that you do not need anyone to feel full; you do not depend on looking for love, how others see you or how their needs and dependencies react. All this implies the realization of an essential exercise of self-esteem, self-improvement, and the search for one's values because you can only love yourself when you know who you are.

"The better you get along with yourself, the better your life is, it doesn't depend on how others perceive you."

-Ana Moreno-

You don't need anyone to complete you

You are enough; you don't need anyone to complete you. Your partner can help you be better than you are, to get the best out of you. Together you can launch a simple life project; you can grow together. But if you depend on your partner and your partner depends on you, you are condemned to drag each other down.

Love will not come into your life from anyone's hand, but you will attract it when it is born of yourself.

Knowing you are enough to create love in your life will prevent you from wasting efforts on such useless actions as living trying to please others or acting on the wishes and aspirations of others. Trying to be another person does not make you or the other person happy, even if you think so. If your priority is to make the other person happy, without thinking about your exact needs, you will see that in the end, you feel even more empty and incomplete.

www.ingramcontent.com/pod-product-compliance
Lightning Source LLC
Chambersburg PA
CBHW070903080526
44589CB00013B/1170